PRAYING
WITH THE
SAINTS

JULIAN OF NORWICH
FRANCIS OF ASSISI

Ernest E. Atkinson
325 Raintree Drive #50
Tyler, TX 75703

Reclaiming the Sacred
PRAYING WITH THE SAINTS

Julian of Norwich
&
Francis of Assisi

Jerry Moye

PEAKE ROAD
Macon, Georgia

ISBN 1-57312-036-7

Praying with the Saints
Julian of Norwich & Francis of Assisi

Jerry Moye

Copyright © 1996
Peake Road
6316 Peake Road
Macon, Georgia 31210-3960
1-800-747-3016

Peake Road
is an imprint of
Smyth & Helwys Publishing, Inc.®

Library of Congress Cataloging-in-Publication Data

Moye, Jerry.
    Praying with the saints:
    Julian of Norwich & Francis of Assisi/
    Jerry Moye.
    x + 118 pp.   6" x 9" (15 x 23 cm.)
    (Reclaiming the sacred)
    Includes bibliographical references.
    ISBN 1-57312-036-7 (alk. paper)
    1. Julian, of Norwich, b. 1343.
    2. Francis, of Assisi, Saint, 1182–1226.
    I. Title. II. Series.
    BV5095.J84M69   1996
    248.3'2—dc20   95-48126
                                                    CIP

CONTENTS

✂ Julian of Norwich ✂

Chapter 1: Called to a Reflective Life

Chapter 2: Prayer as Yearning

Chapter 3: Prayer as Questioning

Chapter 4: Prayer as Confidence

Chapter 5: Praying with Julian Today

❧ Francis of Assisi ❧

PREFACE

During the twenty years I lived in Hong Kong as a Southern Baptist missionary, I was befriended by two great souls: Francis and Julian. Francis lived in twelfth-century Italy, and Julian lived in fourteenth-century England. Both lived in the time of the undivided Western church, although there were rich currents and counter currents present. Both forsook the glamour of worldly careers and longed to hide themselves in Christ, but now they have acquired a mystique.

Francis and Julian have enriched my life immeasurably, as they have helped me probe more deeply who is the Christ. Who is this God-Man who invites us to find him in scripture and church and world? Both saints had a rich personal relationship with Christ, yet both hungered for a deeper identification with him. For some time I have felt that the Pauline longing found in Philippians 3:10 is an apt description of their deepest passion:

> I want to know Christ and the power of his resurrection and the sharing of his sufferings by becoming like him in his death, if somehow I may attain the resurrection from the dead.

Reared as a Baptist, I have had thorough exposure to the Bible but little exposure to church history and the examples of great saints from the past. I have found in myself and many other evangelicals a hunger to know more of our rich Christian heritage. During the Hong Kong missionary years, through Anglican friends and courses I taught in spirituality, I became aware of "the great cloud of witnesses" who span two millennia. Without doubt, Saint Francis and Lady Julian have been my two favorite prayer saints. They have given me a depth to understanding the Bible, as I see how they tried to appropriate scripture for their time and situation. Both are deeply christocentric and warmly human.

I have given several quotations from the primary works of Francis and Julian so that the reader may feel firsthand the uniqueness of their styles. With Francis it is impossible to separate fact from legend, as he has inspired countless people. Stories from *The Little Flowers* reveal not only information about him, but also about his first disciples and interpreters.

Because the two saints lived in a medieval era, it is necessary to give some background information. While we cannot and would not choose to enter totally into their worlds, they offer suggestions to us of recovering things we have lost. I am impressed that the medieval saint did not expect instant gratification of basic religious needs and had rich ways to probe the passion of Christ. I am warned to blend my private struggle of faith with the greater mothering church, rich in experience and need. The greater church needs each of her individual sons and daughters, and we, the individual children, need her.

I dedicate this work to two congregations that have given me a home and place of service since returning to the United States: Baptist Church of the Covenant in Birmingham, Alabama, and University Baptist Church of Montevallo, Alabama. These kindly souls have encouraged me to share my great love for Julian and Francis.

TERMINOLOGY

Examen is a way for a person to discern how God is speaking in past and present experiences. Saint Ignatius Loyola used a method of daily examen to develop in his community a discerning way of life. Noticing and becoming aware of God's presence daily requires an ongoing examining of one's life.

Lectio Divina, or divine reading, is a form of meditation, a slow, prayerful reading of the Scriptures or a passage of inspired writing. We can learn much from those persons past and present who follow this ancient practice of listening and integration. By reading the text slowly several times, word by word, and listening more carefully for the Spirit's voice, the reader enters into and is surrounded by the text. Traditionally, one monk would read a piece of scripture aloud. Silence would follow. The text would be read again, and again. When the listeners had *heard* the text, they would leave and spend time in prayer and silence.

Selah is a term that appears in the body of the Psalms and has as its root meaning "sigh" or "meditate." Some scholars say that the word refers to a pause in the singing for meditation. Others say that it is connected with rising or lifting. Still others say that the word instructed the congregation to cease singing to allow time for worshipers to show God a response or act of worship. Readers are encouraged to pause when the word "selah" appears at the end of each beginning quotation. It prepares them for a prayerful reading of what follows.

JULIAN OF NORWICH

❧ 1 ❧

CALLED TO A REFLECTIVE LIFE

CULTIVATING A LIFE OF HOLINESS

O God, you are my God, I seek you, my soul thirsts for you; my flesh faints for you, as in a dry and weary land where there is no water. So I have looked upon you in the sanctuary, beholding your power and glory. Because your steadfast love is better than life, my lips will praise you. So I will bless you as long as I live; I will lift up my hands and call on your name. My soul is satisfied as with a rich feast, and my mouth praises you with joyful lips when I think of you on my bed, and meditate on you in the watches of the night; for you have been my help, and in the shadow of your wings I sing for joy. My soul clings to you; your right hand upholds me. (Ps 63:1-8)

I remember the days of old, I think about all your deeds, I meditate on the works of your hands. I stretch out my hands to you; my soul thirsts for you like a parched land. (Ps 143:5-6)

Selah

Psalms 63 and 143 provide an uncanny description of a devout woman who had special visions of God, treasured them, and probed their meaning. She is called Lady Julian of Norwich, better known as Mother Julian in her native England. She was an anchoress who lived in the latter half of the fourteenth century. We know of her through two texts that give record of special revelations she had from God. The Early Text is the earliest record of her revelations. The Later Text gives added commentary, the fruit of twenty years of contemplating the special gift of God's "showings."

We do not know Julian's given name. She is called Lady Julian because she was the woman who lived in the anchorhood of the Church of St. Julian outside Norwich. There were three ways a medieval woman could live a holy life under vows administered by the church. She could live under the vow of holy matrimony, be a nun who lived in community with other nuns, or be an anchoress, a woman who lived alone and was dedicated to a life of prayer. Our unnamed saint was called to the life of an anchoress.

An anchoress usually lived in a room or a suite of rooms attached to a church. Julian entered her sacred enclosure, never to leave again. In some places, the anchoress was dedicated to her special life of prayer by a requiem mass, a mass for the dead who leave this world to enter the next. She had limited contacts with the outside world.

One window or squint would enable the anchoress to see the priest in the adjoining sanctuary celebrate mass each day. One squint would enable her to receive food from her servant companion and to hear him speak to her. One squint, covered carefully by a double curtain, would allow people in the area to come to the holy woman for counseling. It was understood, of course, that the anchoress had only set times that she could receive visitors. Her primary work was to live within the daily disciplines of prayer and meditation.

Such a lifestyle may seem strange or even unhealthy to some modern Christians, particularly those who are committed to struggling in the public arena for justice. It was not, however, incomprehensible to the medieval person. The Catholic Church had always honored the ways of Mary and Martha, the sisters who served Jesus. The interpretation arose that Martha helped Jesus by her practical service in the world. Mary, who sat at the feet of Jesus, became a paradigm for the contemplative, and she chose a high calling.

Indeed, the life of Julian would have seemed blessed in many ways to some medieval women. Most women, before the advent of modern birth control, had large families and were burdened with providing for many children with very limited means. A nun or an anchoress was free from the hard burdens of caring for large families. These holy women enjoyed enormous prestige and were often counselors for the humble and great of the land. Julian did not have to worry about

4

food or shelter, so she had maximum opportunity to cultivate the inner life.

We do not know when Julian made the decision to become an anchoress. It seems likely, however, that her encounter with death and the overwhelming gift of revelations—which she admitted she did not yet fully understand—would have made the life of an anchoress seem ideal to her. She would have a way to act out her gratitude and desire for holy service; she would have the ideal circumstances to ponder and grow in understanding of her special revelations through a life dedicated to God in prayer.[1]

Lectio Divina

O God, you are my God, I seek you, my soul thirsts for you; my flesh faints for you, as in a dry and weary land where there is no water. So I have looked upon you in the sanctuary, beholding your power and glory. Because your steadfast love is better than life, my lips will praise you. (Ps 63:1-3)

Examen

How can you best cultivate a life of holiness in your present situation? Notice and become aware of how God's presence is made known to you. One way God spoke to Julian was in visions or dreams. Julian is quick to point out, however, that each person communes with God in his or her own way.

I am not good because of the revelations, but only if I love God better; and inasmuch as you love God better, it is more to you than to me. . . . for we are all one in love, for truly it was not revealed to me that God loves me better than the humblest soul who is in a state of grace. For I am sure that there are many who never had revelations or visions, but only the common teaching of Holy Church, who love God better than I. (LT, 191)[2]

Ask the Lord for the gift you desire.

Closing Meditation

Then our good Lord put a question to me: "Are you well satisfied that I suffered for you?" I said: "Yes, good Lord, all my thanks to you; yes, good Lord, blessed may you be." Then Jesus our good Lord said: "If you are satisfied, I am satisfied. It is a joy, a bliss, an endless delight to me that ever I suffered my Passion for you; and if I could suffer more, I should suffer more." (LT, 216)

A CONTEMPLATIVE
IN OUR MIDST

Embrace the whole world with the arms of your love and in that act at once consider and congratulate the good, contemplate and mourn over the wicked. . . . look upon the afflicted and the oppressed and feel compassion for them. . . . call to mind the wretchedness of the poor, the groan of the orphans, the abandonment of widows, the gloom of the sorrowful. . . . In your love take them all to your heart, weep over them, offer your prayers for them. (Aelred Rule)[3]

Selah

From the *Aelred Rule* we receive an understanding of the scope and attitude of anchorite prayer. We can only speculate why Julian felt called out of ordinary life to this extraordinary life of an anchoress. She became seriously ill when she was thirty years old and faced death. Her family had sent for the priest to administer the last rites of her church. Within a period of thirty hours, Julian had a series of sixteen visions, which she called showings or "shewings." They were revelations of the love of God.

Though Julian was hidden from the world, enclosed in her room attached to the Church of St. Julian, the people of Norwich were very much aware that a holy woman lived in their midst. It was comforting to know that she prayed for them and spent much of her life communing with God. It gave their city a special grace. While she gave primary attention to contemplation and prayer, she still had time to counsel the many persons in need of spiritual encouragement.

We have record of Julian being visited by Margery Kemp. Margery and Julian are a study of contrasts. Margery wrestled with a notion held by many women of her age that the "stain of marriage" prevented her from having a wholehearted love relationship for God. She worked herself into the belief that God had restored her virginity, even though she already had given birth to fourteen children. The Church had always seen marriage as a holy institution, and it blessed large families that increased Mother Church. Yet many saw celibacy as a higher form of piety, including Margery Kemp.[4]

We know from Kemp's book that Julian was keenly intelligent and sensitive to human feelings. Margery said that she was greatly comforted by Mother Julian. What was the substance of Julian's teaching? She did not speak of one's individual choice to be married or celibate. One could love God in either state. She was always deeply christocentric. At the heart of all devotion was wonder and praise of Christ, the courteous Lord.

The Contemplative Life of an Anchoress

An anchoress had more freedom than a nun, as she was not under the constant direction of a supervisor, neither bishop nor mother superior. While she was given instruction, she had much latitude in interpreting her Rule. We have accounts by some church officials that some anchoresses took too many liberties. One was scolded for keeping cows on the village common. Poverty was not one of the vows taken by anchoresses, though most did enter a life of extreme simplicity.

We have copies of some Rules provided for the anchorite life. One is called the *Ancrene Riwle* (Anchor Rule), written by an anonymous author in the thirteenth century for three sisters who had chosen this holy life. Another Rule was provided by Aelred of Rievaulx for his anchoress sister in about 1160; we shall refer to it as the *Aelred Rule*.

The *Ancrene Riwle* has several interesting warnings and suggestions. There are comments on meeting the basic human needs of food, sleep, and clothing. In regard to eating, most people in religious orders followed the general guide of Saint Benedict. A person was allowed one pound of bread and one pint of wine per day. Of course, there were special days of fasting. The *Ancrene Riwle* spoke of fasting every Friday and had this stipulation: "Ye shall eat no flesh nor lard except in great sickness; or whosoever is infirm may eat potage without scruple." While the diet was certainly simple enough, the Rule warned anchoresses not to take on extra fasting and hurt the body.

Sleep for extended periods of time was uncommon to those persons in orders. The twenty-four-hour day was broken up frequently by prayer times. It was understood that many would probably have a siesta in the afternoon and rest periods when needed. The Rule suggests that one is to use sleep as a time of total relaxation, not as a time of continuing the holy work of prayer.

Warnings are given for the anchorite counselors. It was understood that men and women would be drawn to these anchorhoods, seeking comfort from women who spent so much time communing with God. The Rule stipulates that a double curtain is always to be drawn when visitors come. It may not be pulled back, as it would encourage an intimacy that should not be fostered. Anchoresses were to be particularly careful in counseling men. If the men seemed unduly distressed or aggressive in their interviews, they were to be turned away.

An anchoress had a special responsibility for the guidance of her servant companion. She was to exercise careful discipline so that her servant would reflect to the world something of the piety of her mistress. The companion should always be rebuked tenderly. It was wrong to nurse a history of grievances. The temptation for idle gossip was to be avoided.

The *Aelred Rule* provided a timetable for set prayers, the Holy Office. Julian could have heard the chiming of the hours from the great cathedral tower in Norwich and regulated her life by this regular occurrence. The Holy Office, accepted by most members of religious orders, divided the day into seven prayer periods.

Matins came soon after midnight. *Lauds* came with the dawn, followed by *Prime*. *Terce* was at 9:00 in the morning. *Sext* was at noon. *None* was at 3:00 in the afternoon. *Vespers* came in the early evening, followed by *Compline* at bedtime. Following a lectionary, a person had a balanced reading of scriptures that centered primarily on the Psalms and Gospel readings. There were some adjustments to the schedule, as some of the prayer times were combined into a single time. Prayers such as The Lord's Prayer and Hail, Mary were always included.

Lectio Divina

But I call upon God, and the LORD will save me. Evening and morning and at noon I utter my complaint and moan, and he will hear my voice. Cast your burden on the Lord, and he will sustain you; he will never permit the righteous to be moved. (Ps 55:16-17, 22)

Examen

Pay close attention to God's presence in the midst of your responsibilities and activities today and throughout the week. Are you inviting God to be with you? How is God inviting you to be a more prayerful presence to those around you?

Ask the Lord for the gift you desire.

Closing Meditation

Then prayer is a witness that the soul wills as God wills, and it eases the conscience and fits man for grace. And so he teaches us to pray and to have firm trust that we shall have it; for he beholds us in love, and wants to make us partners in his good will and work. (LT, 243)

WAIT . . . IN PRAYERFUL ATTENTIVENESS

For our courteous Lord wants us to be as familiar with him as heart may think or soul may desire; but let us beware that we do not accept this familiarity so carelessly as to forsake courtesy. (LT, 331)

Selah

The medieval way of piety is doubtlessly unfamiliar to many of us today. Those of us who have been nurtured in a Protestant evangelical faith are suspicious of people who isolate themselves from the world and seem to be of little use to the church or world. To some, it seems that people who follow this type of vocation are either running away from the problems in their own life or those in the world. This, of course, is a risk taken when the church blesses the ministry of persons who are not religiously active in a visible way.

Perhaps one of the great strengths of the contemplative life is in its being so countercultural. It is not the obvious way to attain success, working for God or one's boss. For those of us who are active in the world, however, we can find comfort in knowing we are held before God by another human being who has made time to remember us. We are then reminded that we too must find those private and quiet times to renew our energy in prayer. In framing the matter this way, I reveal my own tendency to be a spiritual activist, for the contemplative would sometimes seek times to be with God for God's sake.

Julian stimulates us to probe at least three issues: (1) the healthiness of asceticism, (2) the place of rules for piety, and (3) the reality of religious dreams or visions. I still recall a university history teacher lecturing on early Christian saints and speaking in particular of Saint Simeon Stylites who sat on a raised pillar for thirty-six years in meditation. No interpretation was given, other than this was a case of the extreme lengths early ascetics were willing to endure.

The desert fathers and mothers cannot be dismissed lightly. They were reacting to a church that was beginning to be too comfortable with the status quo. In prophetic, dramatic gesture they pointed to a life of sacrifice and yearning for union with God. Perhaps it would be useful to compare the ascetic practices of the contemplatives to the training of athletes. Spiritual directors constantly reminded their charges that a body satiated with food, sleep, fulfilled goals, and pleasure had little room left for God.

If we respond to the pull of God's love and invitation to enter Jesus' kind of suffering—healing love—we are called to a life of constant discovery, growth, crucifixion, and resurrection. Contemplatives starved the body to feast the soul. This brings us to the matter of following rules. Contemplatives such as Julian followed the discipline of Holy Office to set up new rhythms in their psyche.

How does one follow the biblical injunction to pray without ceasing? One way is to set up a schedule so that every few hours of the day are punctuated by conscious efforts to pray. It should not seem strange that many individuals who have lived in orders know so many psalms by memory that their speaking on religious subjects is unconsciously full of scriptural references from the Gospels. While most of us do not have the built-in mechanism of a cloistered life, we can find ways to punctuate the day frequently with prayer.

Our prayer times do not have to be long or elaborate. During breaks at the office or during a lunch hour in the park, we can meditate on a few choice scriptures or prayers. We can create our own lectionary and focus on a set of scriptures and prayers for whatever length of time we desire. One year I was moved to study the Gospel of John every day for several months. Another year I changed my meditation texts monthly. It is exciting to find our own rhythms and methods when we make the conscious effort to be attentive daily.

I find it helpful to conceive of God and Christ in various images. When I pray for Christian friends in Hong Kong, I somehow see the face of Christ in a particular Chinese woman who is radiant with the love of God. In my dreaming of life, there have been scenes in which God is felt pervading a beautiful world. It is good to stock our waking life with memories, stories, and images of God at work. They may become the visions of our dreaming life. All this is material for prayer. As Julian has instructed, it is not important to have unusual revelations. We draw as close to the Christ of the Gospels as we can, and he provides enlightenment as he will.

In Psalm 62 we find words that well express the faith of Julian. Her faith is in God, who rewards the beloved—those who wait in prayerful attentiveness to see God's goodness are not "greatly moved" in this world.

Lectio Divina

For God alone my soul waits in silence; from him comes my salvation. He only is my rock and my salvation, my fortress; I shall never be shaken. For God alone my soul waits in silence, for my hope is from him. He alone is my rock and my salvation, my fortress; I shall not be shaken. On God rests my deliverance and my honor; my mighty rock, my refuge is in God. (Ps 62:1-2, 5-7)

Examen

For everything which our good Lord makes us to beseech he himself has ordained for us from all eternity. . . . he truly revealed in all these sweet words, where he says "I am the foundation." And our good Lord wants this to be known by his lovers on earth. (LT, 248-9)

Begin your time of prayer in silence. Be attentive to what the Lord is impressing on your heart. Notice your response. If you like, ask the Lord for the meaning of the words, "I am the foundation." Wait . . . in prayerful attentiveness. Ask the Lord for the gift you desire.

Closing Meditation

And so I saw most surely that it is quicker for us and easier to come to the knowledge of God than it is to know our own soul. For our own soul is so deeply grounded in God and so endlessly treasured that we cannot come to knowledge of it until we first have knowledge of God, who is the Creator to whom it is united. (LT, 288)

Notes

[1]Two excellent studies of the life and times of Julian are the following: Brant Pelphrey, "Christ Our Mother, Julian of Norwich," *The Way of the Christian Mystics,* vol. 7 (Wilmington DE: Michael Glazier, Inc., 1989); Grace Jantzen, *Julian of Norwich: Mystic and Theologian* (London: SPCK, 1987).

[2]All quotations to the text of Julian are from the following: "Julian of Norwich Showings," in *The Classics of Western Spirituality,* trans. Edmund Colledge and James Walsh (New York: Paulist Press, 1978). Unless otherwise noted, references are always to the Long or Later Text (LT). Citations will be indicated as LT.

[3]For a discussion of anchorite rules, see Jantzen, *Julian of Norwich,* 28-48. For direct reading of the rules, see the following: "Rule of Aelred of Rievaulx," in *Treatises and the Pastoral Prayer of Cistercian Fathers Series* (Kalamazoo MI: Cisterician Publications, 1971); *The Ancrene Riwle,* ed. James Morton (Boston: John Luce, 1907).

[4]For a discussion of Margery Kemp, see Jantzen, *Julian of Norwich,* 157-58. For Kemp's own account, see *The Book of Margery Kempe,* trans. B. A. Windeatt (New York: Penguin Books, 1985).

2

PRAYER AS YEARNING

YEARNING OF THE SOUL

For this is the loving yearning of the soul through the touch of the Holy Spirit, from the understanding I have in this revelation: God, in your goodness give me of yourself, for you are enough for me, and I can ask for nothing which is less which can pay you full worship. And if I ask anything which is less, always I am in want; but only in you do I have everything. (LT, 184)

Selah

Julian discerns in her revelations the mutual longings of God and God's creatures. While she never states that God was forced to create a world out of loneliness, she does state that God longs for the love of God's world. This is an important point. God chooses to create and to love. No force is greater than God; God indeed is sovereign. Once God decided to create a world, however, a bond was created between the Creator and creation. Since love requires our free assent, God must allow room for us to respond. This evokes longing in God, for God must wait for our understanding to grow, our wills to choose, and our spirits to commune.

We learn from Julian an important aspect of prayer. If God lives with longing, why should we demand instant gratification of our desires? Indeed, God and we must live with longing if love is the life we choose. Patience then is a cardinal virtue in prayer. We wait while nurturing relationships. It takes time and experience for lovers to build a foundation of trust and familiarity. Through obstacles that must be overcome, through testing, lovers learn how to enable each other.

Courtesy becomes another cardinal virtue in prayer. We treat with respect the presence of the other, knowing that we cannot force another's love. Julian envisions God exactly in this way: God is a courteous Lord, patient and hopeful. Though our courteous lover is God, not subject to all our limitations, God has chosen the limitation to offer love and is enriched when we draw near in prayer.

This yearning for God is connected to a partial fulfillment. We are dealing with a paradox: we can have God, and we can never have God. God is the one who awakens us to love, fills us with love, and calls us in endless longing for love. We respond to such love through prayer and service. The more we spend time with God, the more we realize the reality of this partial fulfillment in prayer. Patience and courtesy are needed in prayer as we find God and yet desire God more deeply.

Because Julian had experienced the love of God, she longed to deepen this reality. She was aware that her revelations of love were accommodated to her mortal frame, but they still connected her in an electrifying way to God. Humans, however, are not the controlling or initiating agents of love. We cannot claim to have the infallible way to make God always present according to our timetables and agendas. All mature saints speak of a dark night of the soul, of dry periods of prayer, of feelings of desertion or emptiness. Julian accepted the dry periods and the times without visions, as well as the times of beautiful revelations.

She provides a wise safeguard for careless evangelists who promise immediate gratification for deep basic needs and who imply there is a way to possess infinite God. Julian also gives us a view that is contrary to the values of our consumer age. We can easily be misled to believe there is a quick fix for every problem or instant gratification for every need. The longing for a vital relationship with God, however, is not met quickly by guaranteed methods of knowing the right techniques or having the correct answers.

God chooses to work through methods of prayer and concepts of religion, but God is not limited to our frantic struggle with these. We learn to do prayers of silence as well as articulation. We learn to offer up our longings as well as our prayers of thanksgiving for what we have experienced. We accept the pain of longing, for it also is joy.

16

Loving yearning of the soul awakens in us a desire for a deeper identification with God. It leads us to go deep down into the soul with its memories and perceptions, and like Julian we find that God is there. Longing prayer also leads us to look out into the world and marvel at the smallest part of God's creation, the hazelnut. And again we discover, God is there. God showed Julian that "it lasts and always will, because God loves it; and thus everything has being through the love of God."

Lectio Divina

As a deer longs for flowing streams, so my soul longs for you, O God. My soul thirsts for God, for the living God. When shall I come and behold the face of God? (Ps 42:1-2)

Examen

Thank the Lord for giving you the desire to be in His presence. How will you respond to such beseeching love?

And our Lord said, "I am the ground of your beseeching. First, it is my will that you should have it, and then I make you to wish it, and then I make you to beseech it. If you beseech it, how could it be that you would not have what you beseech?" (LT, 248)

Ask the Lord for the gift you desire.

Closing Meditation

I saw three kinds of longing in God, and all to the same end, and we have the same in us, and from the same power, and for the same end. The first is because he longs to teach us to know him and to love him always more and more, as is suitable and profitable to us. The second is that he longs to bring us up into bliss, as souls are when they are taken out of pain into heaven. The third is to fill us with bliss, and that will be fulfilled on the last day, to last forever. (LT, 326)

DESIRE FOR THREE GIFTS AND THREE WOUNDS

*The creature (Julian) had desired three graces by the gift of God.
The first was recollection of the Passion. The second was bodily
sickness. The third was to have, of God's gifts, three wounds. (LT,
177)*

*By the grace of God and the teaching of Holy Church, I conceived
a great desire to receive three wounds in my life, that is, the
wound of true contrition, the wounds of loving compassion, and
the wound of longing with my will for God. (LT, 178-2)*

Selah

J ulian carefully dates the time she received her revelations: "This revelation was made to a simple, unlettered creature, living in this
mortal flesh of our Lord 1373, on the thirteenth day of May." (LT,
177) She states that she was thirty and one-half years-old, afflicted
with a great bodily sickness, when she received the visions. As she
begins to write down her revelations, she recalls the special prayers of
her pious youth.

Long ago Julian had made two special requests, knowing they
should be conditional, for only God could know if they were good
requests. She later remembered that she had made a third request: to
receive from the Lord three kinds of spiritual wounds. Throughout her
life she had desired God to give her the three spiritual wounds, but
Julian forgot about the earlier two requests. Her prayer would be
answered in 1373.

Though such prayer requests may seem strange to us, they are
understandable in Julian's time. She would have seen beautiful paintings of the crucified Jesus in the prosperous churches of Norwich.
Often the paintings showed women at the foot of the cross of Jesus,
women such as Mary the mother and Mary Magdalene. Julian was

deeply christocentric. She rejoiced in Christ's humanity and longed to identify with his physical suffering.

As to her second request, desiring a serious bodily illness, Julian recalled that she hoped the experience would come in her thirtieth year. She believed a serious illness would take away all the cushioning she had received from her family and church. This, she thought, would provide a greater opportunity to trust God alone and to know without doubt that God was healer and Lord. Julian's request was logical, but she knew it was an unusual one. She added that it was a conditional request: only God could decide if the request was wise.

Why should Julian desire the illness by age thirty? Life expectancy was not long in the fourteenth century. It was the century of the Black Death that wiped out a large part of the population. Many women, pregnant during most of their childbearing years, died while giving birth. We do not know if Julian had been married or widowed, or if she remained single, but no one took a long life as guaranteed. By age thirty, one should have had the major experiences that life could afford.

Julian's third request, like the second, was a natural outworking of the first. A Christian does not desire to ponder the crucifixion of Christ as an idle exercise. A zealous Christian such as Julian wanted to share the pain and love of Christ. A literal seeking of crucifixion would be ridiculous, but we can bear inner pain as we live for Christ's cause.

How interesting it is to see the way Julian interpreted the pain or cost of discipleship! In her eyes, discipleship is related to contrition, compassion, and yearning. It begins with sorrow and turning from sin, from all that keeps the soul from drawing close to the pure and loving Lord.

She never believed she would reach perfection in this life, but she would always do enough self-examination to expose her weaknesses to the light of God. If she were pure like Christ, she would share the compassionate nature of Christ. Drawing close to God meant drawing closer to those around her. Each request in prayer came out of the deepest yearnings of love.

19

Lectio Divina

We are afflicted in every way, but not crushed; perplexed, but not in despair; perplexed, but not driven to despair; persecuted but not forsaken; struck down, but not destroyed; always carrying in the body the death of Jesus, so that the life of Jesus may also be made visible in our bodies. For while we live, we are always being given up to death for Jesus' sake, so that the life of Jesus may be made visible in our mortal flesh. (2 Cor 4:8-11)

Examen

Recall a time in your life when you felt identified in some way with Christ. You might want to spend time in prayer, asking the Lord to bring to mind a time when you have shared His "passion." These "wounds" strengthen your faith.

Some wounds, however, need to be entrusted to the Lord for healing. Perhaps someone or something has wounded you in the past, and you still carry the hurt with you. Are you willing to face the hurt—the person(s), institutions, lost dreams, or compromises—with Christ?

Ask the Lord for the gift you desire.

Closing Meditation

Pity and love protect us in the time of our need; and the longing in the same love draws us into heaven, for God's thirst is to have man, generally, drawn into him, and in that thirst he has drawn his holy souls who are now in bliss. And so, getting his living members, always he draws and drinks, and still he thirsts and he longs. (LT, 326)

A CALL TO PERSEVERE

Our Lord is most glad and joyful because of our prayer; and he expects it, and he wants to have it, for with his grace it makes us like to himself in condition as we are in nature, and such is his blessed will. . . . Pray wholeheartedly, though you may feel nothing, though you may see nothing, yes, though you think you could not, for in dryness and in barrenness, in sickness and in weakness, then is your prayer most pleasing to me, though you think it almost tasteless to you. (LT, 249)

Selah

These words are characteristic of Julian's pastoral concern and practical wisdom. As a wise spiritual counselor, she calls us to a disciplined prayer life. We become more fulfilled in prayer, since we are like God "in nature." While sin is the constant problem for union with God, we are made for fellowship with our Creator and can cooperate with God to fulfill our created nature. A person becomes what he or she thinks, focuses on, and chooses. A Christian who remains constant in prayer becomes more and more "oned" with Christ.

Julian has rich passages that speak of the priority of God in prayer. Behind our longings and efforts is the previous moving of God. In her fourteenth revelation Julian wishes to encourage those who feel defeated in prayer. She mentions the problems of believing the soul is too unworthy to approach God and not feeling any obvious kind of emotional warmth. With or without emotional glow, one should always pray. God is always present; our very desire, despite the lack of emotion, is proof of that. Since God is the ground of our desire, we can persevere through God's endless resources.

"You Will Not Be Overcome"

Julian had awakened between the fifteenth and final revelation for a short while. She spoke to her priest about her "ravings." Her priest, a pious man, took holy dreams seriously and did not share her lighthearted comments. She felt guilty that she had not seemed to pay proper respect for her revelations. She fell back into sleep, and in her last revelation fought with the devil. He was conceived in full medieval imagery: he had red hair, a long freckled face, the paws of a beast, and a foul smell.

Julian was comforted, however, by a vision of the Lord Jesus. He sat in the citadel of her soul, resplendent in glory and full of courteous concern. He told her that her vision was true and gave her these words of assurance: "You will not be overcome." She understood that she would continue to struggle with her sin and imperfection, but she would be greatly enabled by a life of devotion. The marvelous gift of the revelations provided special means to cultivate a holy life, which necessarily requires faithful determination.

There was a popular story known to Julian and all of her generation about a holy woman who bore three wounds for Christ. She refers to it briefly in the Short Text of her *Revelations*. It is the story of Saint Cecilia, remembered as an early Christian martyr who faithfully persevered to the very end. Cecilia was a devout woman who had secretly decided to dedicate her life as a virgin to Christ. Her non-Christian father married her to a non-Christian Roman. Cecilia so pleaded with her husband to remain chaste that he agreed and was even converted. The husband and his brother paid a terrible price for their faith. They were martyred.

Since Cecilia was seen as the corrupting influence on noble Roman youth, she was given a specially severe penalty. She was to be boiled alive. Miraculously she survived, and the soldiers decided to behead her. Miraculously again, she survived for a long while. The soldier had tried three times to decapitate Cecilia, but he could not completely sever the neck tendons. It was illegal for an executioner to strike four times, so she was left to bleed to death. For three days Cecilia bore radiant witness to her faith. Finally she died, received her martyr's crown, and has inspired the saints ever since. Such stories were wonderful to the medieval imagination and obviously inflamed the heart of the young Julian to stand firm.

God's Praise for Perseverance

Julian explored the joy of God's appreciation of God's servants. There were three degrees of bliss for a faithful servant: (1) God personally thanked those who were faithful and endured such hardship on earth. (2) Everyone in God's banqueting hall would see the honor God gave her, and this would increase her pleasure. (3) God's joy in God's servants was everlasting. God particularly praised those who were faithful servants since youth.

We cannot know what Julian is referring to, but we remember she spoke of the devotion of her youth in seeking three gifts and three wounds. In her sixth revelation, Julian sees God, the rejoicing knight, at a banquet in a heavenly house. God entertained graciously, making everyone glad and merry. God provided wonderful music and deeply enjoyed the guests. God then said to Julian: "I thank you for your service and your labour in your youth."

Julian speaks of the priority of God's moving us in love to yearn for God and warns that we must not worry about dryness or other difficulties in prayer. She encourages Christians to persevere in prayer, for she knew that some prayers would require a long and patient wait before her courteous Lord would answer.

Lectio Divina

So I will bless you as long as I live; I will lift up my hands and call on your name. My soul is satisfied as with a rich feast, and my mouth praises you with joyful lips when I think of you on my bed, and meditate on you in the watches of the night; for you have been my help, and in the shadow of your wings I sing for joy. My soul clings to you; your right hand upholds me. (Ps 63:4-8)

Examen

Do you have a prayer request, a relationship, or a life situation that requires perseverance? How has the Lord responded? How have you responded? Find encouragement in Julian's spiritual counsel:

Pray wholeheartedly, though you may feel nothing, though you may see nothing, yes, though you think you could not, for in dryness and in barrenness, in sickness and in weakness, then is your prayer most pleasing to me, though you think it almost tasteless to you. (LT, 249)

Ask the Lord for the gift you desire.

Closing Meditation

And so he moves us to pray for what it pleases him to do, and for this prayer and good desire which come to us by his gift he will repay us, and give us eternal reward. And this was revealed to me when he said: "If you beseech it." In this saying God showed such great pleasure and such great delight as though he were much beholden to us for each good deed that we do; and yet it is he who does it. (LT, 243)

ᥴᥬ3ᥬᥱ
Prayer as Questioning

"Something . . . I Need to Know"

It is something which I need to know . . . if I shall live here, so as to tell good from evil, whereby I may through reason and grace separate them more distinctly, and love goodness and hate evil . . . I cried within me with all my might, beseeching God for help, in this fashion: "Ah, Lord Jesus, king of bliss, how shall I be comforted, who will tell me and teach me what I need to know, if I cannot at this time see it in you?" (LT, 266-7)

Selah

Julian's vision of God always had love, marked by sovereign courtesy, as its main focus. Julian had no revelation of God's wrath nor of hell. She was gentle, intelligent, and highly sensitive to all the movements of a love relationship. Her God was of the same nature. Julian, however, was obedient to the teachings of mother church.

The Church had taught her that we all are sinners, deserving God's wrath. Morality plays, legends, and pictures—which depicted a darker side of religion—adorned the churches. Therefore, Julian had a twofold problem: she did not feel herself to be a rebellious soul resisting the love of God; nor did she have a revelation of God, enraged or ready to act with terrible judgment.

Julian found, in her prayerful probings, the age-old questions of monotheism to be impediments to her confidence. If God were good and all powerful, how do we explain the presence of evil? Is it created by God, allowed by God, or used by God? Is evil so powerful that even

God must step aside and allow it to have its place? If we are caught in its grip, do we have choices and real freedom?

Julian was finally given an answer of some sort in the form of a parable. The parable, however, had multiple levels of meaning and was not immediately understandable. She spent twenty years "less three months" pondering the meaning. The years of her anchorhood provided time and proper environment to tease out the meaning through prayer and reflection. The parable is given in the fourteenth revelation, not found in the Short Text.

A PARABLE
FALL OF THE SERVANT GARDENER

The parable that solved Julian's problem of seeing God's connection to sin is found in Chapter 51 of her Long Text, the longest chapter of her book. It reveals the fruit of years of prayerful probing and is a remarkable piece of fresh theological thinking. Julian presents the basic images and then returns to them again and again for every possible bit of meaning.

Pelphrey, a Julian scholar and friend of mine who has discussed Julian's spirituality with me many times, has made a very creative suggestion that her parable is like a medieval morality play. He sketches how the story could have been staged and how medieval onlookers would have responded with laughter and approval.

It would not be the first time that people have found answers to profound questions in dramatic myths or stories. Perhaps these answers speak to our own deep questions. Julian was fascinated by the drama, knowing that it somehow provided answers she desperately needed. To find meaning in the parable, Julian had to apply the hard work of prayerful meditation to the dramatic immediacy of the story she saw in a night.

The story begins with a grand lord, clothed in a brilliant robe of azure blue, sitting on a throne on a flat, empty plain. He is attended by only one servant, dressed in a torn, dirty tunic. The lord sends his servant out on a mission. Later we are told the nature of the mission.

The servant was to uncover a great treasure hidden in the earth. The great treasure was to eat and enjoy the fruits that the earth could produce. The servant then was to be a gardener. He was to labor hard to produce fruit to feed the great lord who desired this service from his servant and the good food of the earth.

The servant was very willing to obey his master. He went out with great zeal to please his lord, but fell into a ditch and was greatly injured. He feared the displeasure of his master, but the great lord looked upon him with great pity. The good lord decided that he would give great honor to his servant once he was out of the pit and returned. He did not desire to punish the servant for his fall. He was moved by his servant's efforts.

The first level of meaning was to see the two figures as God and Adam. There are reminiscences of the Garden of Eden described in Genesis 2 and the parable of the vineyard in Isaiah 5. Julian knew that the figure of the servant represented all humankind and not just a single person.

A PARABLE
GRACE OF THE GOOD LORD

The gardener servant was not by nature an evil person. He did not have the perfection of his master, but he did have the capacity to love the master and try to serve him. His imperfection was in his weakness or frailty, in blindness or partial understanding of the truth, in fearfulness or complete lack of trust in the loving nature of his Lord. He suffered in body the consequences of his fall and would bear the marks of his injuries all his life.

Julian then had a beginning knowledge of the imperfection of humankind and the consistent loving nature of God. Still she needed some explanation of how the gardener was restored. This came later when she saw a second level of application. The gardener who fell was also Jesus Christ. This figure was Adam and the New Adam, the Christ, at the same time. Indeed with further thought it seemed obvious that the good lord knew that his imperfect servant would eventually fall. From the beginning, he had planned that his Christ would fall into human life and experience it fully. Whereas the first Adam failed and unleashed a crippling power on us all, the second Adam, Christ, would succeed and release a renewing power for us all.

> When Adam fell, God's son fell; because of the true union that was made in heaven, God's son could not be separated from Adam, for by Adam I understand all mankind. Adam fell from life to death, into the valley of his wretched world, and after that into hell. God's son fell with Adam, into the valley of the womb of the maiden who was the fairest daughter of Adam, and that was to excuse Adam from blame in heaven and on earth, and powerfully he brought him out of hell. . . . The strength and goodness that we have is from Jesus Christ, the weaknesses and blindness that we have is from Adam, which two were shown in the servant. (LT, 274)

Lectio Divina

[God] does not deal with us according to our sins, nor repay us according to our iniquities. For as the heavens are high above the earth, so great is his steadfast love toward those who fear him; as far as the east is from the west, so far he removes our transgressions from us. (Ps 103:10-12)

Examen

In examining where you are in your journey with God, do you feel more like the fallen servant or the restored gardener? Why?

Ask the Lord for the gift you desire.

Closing Meditation

Ah, Lord Jesus, king of bliss, how shall I be comforted, who will tell me and teach me what I need to know, if I cannot at this time see it in you? . . . And then our courteous Lord answered very mysteriously, by revealing a wonderful example of a lord who has a servant, and gave me sight for the understanding of them both. (LT, 267)

PRAYERFUL PROBING

The lord is God the Father, the servant is the Son, Jesus Christ, the Holy Spirit is the equal love which is in them both. (LT, 274)

Selah

Our image of God shapes the manner in which we relate to God in prayer. Julian must have been keenly aware of this from her own life and from the lives of those she counseled. As Julian wrestled with the parable of the good lord and the servant gardener, she applied the Trinity doctrine. Julian saw God as Father, Son, and Holy Spirit.

Her image of God as Trinity reveals an intelligent sophistication. She avoids the temptation of many Christians to separate the work of God the Father and Jesus. Some make God the Father so one-dimensional in His maintaining honor through exercising wrath that the Son is seen as victim, separate from the Father. God, however, is fully present in Jesus, the Son. The bond that unifies the Father and the Son is the Holy Spirit. In a way, both live in the Spirit as a kind of common ground. The Spirit is the pulling power within God that awakens us in yearning to God.

Julian continues her prayerful probing:

> That is to say, even though he (Christ) is God, equal with the Father as regards his divinity, but with his prescient purpose that he would become man to save mankind in fulfillment of the will of his Father. (LT, 275)

How specifically does Christ, falling into our human condition, save us? He endures all the afflictions of humankind, including the ultimate experience of death. Christ, however, is resurrected, overcoming the power of death and decay. If he is able to break the law of death and decay, a new power is at work in the world. If we are in him, we experience resurrection in him. Julian uses the images of colored robes to depict the lesson.

The great Lord is clothed in a beautiful azure blue garment. The Old Adam is in a tattered, dirty tunic. When the New Adam is raised from the dead, however, he wears a magnificent robe, even more resplendent than that of the Father. It seems to be all the colors of the rainbow, all the colors that come from the refracted light of whiteness: "Christ's clothing is now of a fair and seemly mixture, which is so marvelous that I cannot describe it, for it is all of true glory."

Julian's questions trigger questions in me. How are we to understand our nature? Can I have a worthy faith that has a loving God at the center, one who really can overcome the evil or darker side of experience and integrate all I am into a growing, healthy whole? In facing limitations put on us from birth, does individual effort to get out of the "ditches" we fall into have any hope of success?

Julian has a healthy creation theology. God takes great delight in all creation. It is interesting in her parable that God, the great Lord, desires the cultivation of a garden and looks forward to enjoying the produce of the land. While she spiritualizes the meaning of God hungering and thirsting, she still finds the image of real food and water rich ones to use. God has particular delight in humankind and is depicted as always concerned for the well-being of God's own creatures.

People are God's good creation, but we are not perfect like God. We are flawed, but not rejected. The traditional biblical word for our imperfection is sin. Sin, we know, has many dimensions. Julian had a particular temperament that led her to define sin in a particular way. She was gentle and ready to serve God from her earliest youth. Her sins were not those of inordinate pride, violent temper, raging lust, or grasping for power. She saw sin in terms of frailty, spiritual blindness, and fearfulness. To be sure, these are aspects of sin.

We must supplement our understanding of sin by consulting others. Augustine, whose thought has many points of kinship with Julian, knew sin to include other areas. He was converted late in life, contemptuous of simple Christian thought and tempted by a strong libido. Many persons are afflicted with a deep pride that cannot tolerate any check on private agendas. Julian was so focused on a love relationship with God that she was spared the results of following her own will.

To love fully involves constant enlargement of soul by surrendering a self-contained power center. Julian then teaches us that we are most human when we are most open to love. We are by nature made for love and most fulfilled when we are grounded in God who is love. We are imperfect in love, sinners all, but never lost to God who is powerful love.

We wrestle with a second question: How can God love me, since I am a sinner? Surely God is constantly disappointed, but God loves me because it is God's nature to love. Julian explores this with rich discussion of God as a perfect, loving parent and a perfect, loving spouse. It is interesting to see how Julian understands God to use sin for God's ultimate purpose to bless all creation.

My efforts to come out of the "ditches" I fall into are important. We can cooperate with God as God turns our sin scars into badges of honor. Julian explores the thought of overcoming sin as badges of honor in her thirteenth revelation, a study of sin and forgiveness. She thinks of dramatic examples of great sinners who were redeemed. In the Old Testament there was David, guilty of adultery and maneuvering a faithful soldier into death. In the New Testament there was Mary Magdalene, a figure much discussed in the medieval period as one capable of much love.

Julian has been careful not to call God the originator of evil, though she understands that God is able to use evil ("God allowed him to fall"). God is indeed sovereign goodness, and all things eventually come under God's sway. Though evil does its worst, it cannot displace God. It causes us pain and suffering, but this only throws us onto the mercy of God. Evil and sin are used by God to deepen God's loving relationships with us.

Julian was a radiant person who had a very healthy faith. There is an optimistic quality throughout her book, but we must be careful not to gloss over her struggle. She had intellectual questions that had to be answered. She used all of her resources: the teaching of mother church, scripture, and the lifestyle of an anchoress that provided time and structure for hard thinking or earnest prayer. Often when she is referred to by those who have some knowledge of her, the following quotation is given: "All will be well, and all will be well, and every kind

31

of thing will be well." Such confidence was the fruit of a disciplined prayer life.

Lectio Divina

Therefore, since we are justified by faith, we have peace with God through our Lord Jesus Christ, through whom we have obtained access to this grace in which we stand; and we boast in our hope of sharing the glory of God. (Rom 5:1-2)

Examen

Spend a few moments in silence. Pay attention to what surfaces within you during the time of silence. Bring any questions you may have before the Lord.

And so has our good Lord Jesus taken upon him all our blame; and therefore our Father may not, does not wish to assign more blame to us than to his own beloved son Jesus Christ. (LT, 275)

Ask the Lord for the gift you desire.

Closing Meditation

Sin is necessary, but all will be well, . . . and every kind of thing will be well. . . . And it seems to me that this pain is something for a time, for it purges and makes us know ourselves and ask for mercy. (LT, 225)

❧4❧

PRAYER AS CONFIDENCE

CONFIDENCE IN GOD AS TRUE MOTHER AND FATHER

So Jesus Christ, who opposes good to evil, is our true Mother. We have our being from him, where the foundation of motherhood begins, with all the sweet protection of love which endlessly follows. As truly as God is our Father, so truly God is our Mother, and He revealed that in everything, and especially in these sweet words. (LT, 295)

Selah

Julian had great confidence in God because of the way she understood God's nature. God was a perfect loving parent, a perfect loving spouse, and a perfect loving knight. Julian displays great originality in contemplating God as perfect father and mother. Others, like Anselm and Bernard, broached the subject. Some scriptural texts suggest God has a mothering quality. Julian, however, develops the thought more than most, and her thought is distinctly her own.

In her fourteenth revelation, Julian probes the matter of God as parenting love. The discussion immediately follows the reporting of her vision parable of the good lord and his gardener servant. The image of God as good father is, of course, very familiar to Christians. We also recall, however, that Jesus likened himself to a mother hen gathering her chicks. The door is opened to explore the mothering nature of God as well as God's fathering nature, once we declare that we take all scripture seriously and are unwilling to lose any of its help in understanding the nature of our God.

Julian was not reluctant to expand the notion of God as Mother. What is unusual is that she likened Jesus to our mother. Since the Holy Spirit is not usually strongly identified with masculine or feminine imaging, we might consider speaking of Spirit as the mothering quality of God, but not so for Julian. Her worshiping experience at mass directed her thought; she fed on her Lord as a babe feeds from its mother. The first reference to Christ as Mother is found in the fourteenth revelation.

Jesus is our mother in nature and our mother in grace. Our natural mother feeds us and sustains our being. God as Creator must have that same mothering quality, but Jesus is also the one who feeds us spiritually. As a child feeds at the mother's breast, so we feed from Jesus. With medieval imagination, not embarrassed by talking about the body and its functions, Julian gives this explanation:

> The mother can give her child to suck of her milk, but our precious Mother Jesus can feed us with himself, and does, most courteously and most tenderly. (LT, 298)

Another function of motherhood is encouraging bruised children. When a child falls and hurts herself, the child will probably run to the mother for comfort and aid. The child will not likely run away from the good parent when he needs comfort. For Christians who are hard on themselves in maintaining high standards and do not easily forgive themselves for failure, Julian is an excellent counselor. Many times I have gone to her words as assurance to go to God:

> So he wants us to act as a meek child, saying: My kind Mother, my gracious Mother, have mercy on me. . . . I may not and cannot make it right except with your help and grace. (LT, 301)

Julian feels no reluctance to describe God as Father and Mother and suggests that each one of us should have both fathering and mothering qualities as she gives one of her frequent references to the Trinity:

> For the almighty truth of the Trinity is our Father . . . And the deep wisdom of the Trinity is our Mother, in whom we are enclosed. (LT, 285)

34

Prayer as Confidence

The Trinity is our feeble way to speak of the incredible fullness of God. God is not a static oneness, but a dynamic interplay of love at work. Since we humans are not pure spirit, we can only know of spiritual love as it is grounded and channeled through our bodies. We may be celibate, but the experience of love still moves through our thoughts and feelings enfleshed in bodies. If we are fortunate enough to have loving parents, we know that the love of parents is spiritual, though expressed in countless ways in our earthly experience. Love of father and mother is sacramental, the visible means of an invisible grace.

While it is good for a person to know the special qualities that come from both a good father and a good mother, it is also good that each person have something of both masculine and feminine strength. If God is a combination of fathering and mothering power, each of us made in God's image can be a combination of fathering and mothering power. We each have this combination in varying proportions. How wonderful it would be for our church to help us discern what particular mothering and fathering qualities we possess and to bless us in using our gifts!

Lectio Divina

Yet it was I who taught Ephraim to walk, I took them up in my arms; but they did not know that I healed them. I led them with cords of human kindness, with bands of love. I was to them like those who lift infants to their cheeks. I bent down to them and fed them. (Hos 11:3-4)

Examen

And though our earthly mother may never suffer us who are his children to perish, our heavenly Mother Jesus may never suffer us who are his children to perish, for he is almighty, all wisdom and all love, and so is none but he, blessed may he be. (LT, 301)

Ask the Lord for the gift you desire.

Closing Meditation

And I saw no difference between God and our substance, but, as it were, all God; and still my understanding accepted that our substance is in God, that is to say that God is God, and our substance is a creature in God. For the almighty truth of the Trinity is our Father, for he made us and keeps us in him. And the deep wisdom of the Trinity is our Mother, in whom we are enclosed. (LT, 285)

CONFIDENCE IN GOD AS A COURTEOUS KNIGHT

For I saw no wrath except on man's side, and he forgives that in us, for wrath is nothing else but a perversity and an opposition to peace and to love. And it comes from a lack of power or a lack of wisdom or a lack of goodness, and this lack is not in God, but it is on our side. For we through sin and wretchedness have in us a wrath and a constant opposition to peace and to love. (LT, 262)

Selah

Julian's God is an unfailingly courteous knight and inquires after her welfare often. Interestingly, in her portrait, God—the perfect warrior—has no wrath. God is in such control of God's own nature that we need never fear facing some irrational outburst of rage. This is not to say that God denies the presence of evil and sin, condones wrongdoing, or suffers when we will not turn to God in love. God simply allows evil to run its course, knowing that divine goodness and love are sovereign and cannot be overcome. God may allow God's beloved to fall into sin, but if this does happen, it will eventually deepen their relationship.

Julian's image of God was not that of a wrathful God, unlike many people who picture God as an angry, avenging God. To be sure, Julian would have read many biblical texts of God's indignation from the psalms used in Holy Office. Julian believed deeply, however, that (1) God is in control of God's own nature and responds out of that nature (love), not in emotional outbursts; (2) God's controlling oneness is the desire to *love creation* perfectly; and (3) God's nature is not subject to change. This interpretation stresses the eternal nature of God to always be God.

Imperfect humans, however, may rage in wrath, for we are not perfect in love. In her fourteenth revelation, Julian gives an interesting discussion of wrath and describes the source of its nature as "a lack of wisdom or a lack of goodness . . . a constant opposition to peace and to love" (LT, 262). Theologian Grace Jantzen made the helpful comment that we must not project onto another, including God, our own turbulence and disintegration. Even Julian would never have denied that some persons will endure the pains of hell. She personally had a vision of being faced by a demon who hated her and desired her damnation.

While Julian knew the effects of wrath, she instead centered her prayer life in those images of God that she discerned through the revelations she received. If we use wrath to describe God, we must be careful that we do not sacrifice the primacy of God's love, the base of all, nor impute to God our own uncontrolled rage. Julian must have encountered many persons in spiritual counseling who held images of a God full of wrath. No doubt, she sought to encourage them to approach God in prayer with confidence that they would be received by a loving and courteous friend.

Her vision of God as perfect knight without wrath gave Julian great confidence. She enjoyed the fruits of God's courtesy and never showed disrespect for God. She, like Francis of Assisi, transfigured the medieval concepts of courtly love. They agreed with the troubadours that love always was connected to longing and suffering and ennobled the basest souls. Their understanding of God's love, however, was not confined to the courts of aristocrats and dandies prone to adultery. Julian's very confidence was based on a thankful response for God, whose courtesy was so perfect that God did not lose sovereignty even when graciously giving all for the sake of the beloved.

Julian remembers the words of her courteous knight:

It is a joy, a bliss, an endless delight to me that ever I suffered my Passion for you; and if I could suffer more, I should suffer more. (LT, 216)

Julian reflected, through years of prayer, on Jesus' words:

He did not say: "If it were necessary to suffer more," but: "If I could suffer more"; for although it might not have been necessary, if he could suffer more he would.

Her perfect knight was not fulfilling some responsibility that lay outside his closest desires. He was personally interested in and totally available to his servant. Jesus has joyfully provided the way for us to come before God, and he desires—yea, beseeches—us into his loving presence. How could such a courteous master not inspire supreme confidence, for Julian and for us today?

Lectio Divina

Therefore, my friends, since we have confidence to enter the sanctuary by the blood of Jesus, by the new and living way that he opened for us through the curtain (that is, through his flesh). . . . let us approach with a true heart in full assurance of faith. . . . Let us hold fast to the confession of our hope without wavering, for he who has promised is faithful. (Heb 10:19-23)

Examen

When you approach God in prayer, what is your predominant image of God? Where did this image originate? Does your image instill confidence? Are you open to receive the Lord in a new way?

Closing Meditation

I saw our Lord God as a lord in his own house, who has called all his friends to a splendid feast. Then I did not see him seated anywhere in his own house; but I saw him reign in his house as a king and fill it all full of joy and mirth, gladdening and consoling his dear friends with himself, very familiarly and courteously, with wonderful melody in endless love in his own fair blissful countenance, which glorious countenance fills all heaven full of the joy and bliss of the divinity. (LT, 203)

CONFIDENCE IN GOD AS PERFECT LOVER

And so I saw that God rejoices that he is our Father, and God rejoices that he is our Mother, and God rejoices that he is our true spouse, and that our soul is his beloved wife. (LT, 279)

Selah

Julian stimulates the question of how to deepen our confidence in God and in those we love. For Julian, courtesy is a way of doing love, entering God's own kind of life. I am fascinated by her image of God as a model of courteous love. Such perfect love is related to showing respect for the other. It acknowledges the differences that lie between different people, but finds a gentle way to make the other feel accepted and valuable. Courteous love seems to me to include at least these elements: (1) acknowledging a distance, (2) extending a cordial invitation for the other to be heard, (3) being attentive, and (4) desiring the welfare of the other.

How, then, can we demonstrate courtesy—a way of doing love—when we pray? Courteous lovers do not barge into the presence of God, though there may be times when we as injured children run into God's presence crying. It is good to enter a silence when we begin to pray, removing ourselves from the distractions of the moment and the petitions uppermost in our minds.

Begin in adoration. Then acknowledge God as the ground of our yearning to pray, the power to pray, and God as the ultimate goal of our prayer. While we rejoice in the knowledge that God is known to us in scripture and previous experience, we carefully honor God's majesty, for God is always more than what we understand. In short, we acknowledge the distance that always exists, even when we feel most united with the Lord.

Come into God's presence with thanksgiving. We have been invited to share our concerns. God does not have to receive us, but God has chosen to hear and enjoy our fellowship. As we come to believe that God is truly attentive to us in prayer, we in turn must be attentive to the way the Lord chooses to reveal Himself to us.

God speaks through scripture, so be attentive to God's voice in the ancient texts. Listening to God's voice in scripture does not mean that a person gives mindless obedience to a literal reading of the text nor casually dismisses the wisdom of an earlier time. Do the work of prayer, like Julian, to integrate God's voice of the past with God's voice of the present.

We should be attentive to the Lord's voice in family, friends, and those we come into contact with daily. I have often felt the Lord's presence when reading the work of Julian. When she speaks to fearful, timid souls that God is like a good mother who wants her dirty and injured children to run to God's comforting arms, I know I am hearing God's voice.

Sometimes I hear the Lord's voice in people I do not particularly like. Every human being, however, is made in God's image and has some special way to reveal the mystery of our creation. A person may speak with bluntness or ignorance of my sensitivities, but I may hear from the words some truth of how I cope and what I value. Can we put aside for a moment our immediate reaction to the presence of the other? Can we in courtesy wait and see if God's word, a revealing word, is being given?

If there is no doubt that God loves all creation with such perfect and courteous love, should I love less? Seek to cultivate greater courtesy in dealing with others. Remember that the base of it all is to know life abundant as it flows from the sovereign love of God.

PRAYER AS CONFIDENCE

Lectio Divina

As God's chosen ones, holy and beloved, clothe yourselves with compassion, kindness, humility, meekness, and patience. Bear with one another and, if anyone has a complaint against another, forgive each other; just as the Lord has forgiven you. . . . Above all, clothe yourselves with love, which binds everything together in perfect harmony. And let the peace of Christ rule in your hearts, to which indeed you were called in the one body. (Col 3:12-15)

Examen

In prayerfully reviewing your week, how would you describe your "clothing"? Is there a particular "garment" from the Colossians passage that you need the Lord's help in "putting on?" Colossians 3:15 must have come to mind when Julian reflected on one of her revelations. God showed Julian that her soul rested deep within her heart:

as wide as if it were an endless citadel . . . [and] the place which Jesus takes in our soul he will nevermore vacate, for in us is his home of homes and his everlasting dwelling. (LT, 67)

In order for "the peace of Christ" to "rule in your [heart]," are there any areas in your life you need to surrender to him? Be encouraged by the fact that Jesus will not vacate "his home of homes" in your life.

Ask the Lord for the gift you desire.

Closing Meditation

What, do you wish to know your Lord's meaning in this thing? Know it well, love was his meaning: Who reveals it to you? Love. What did he reveal to you? Love. Why does he reveal it to you? For Love. (LT, 342)

5

PRAYING WITH JULIAN TODAY

"BY NATURE AND BY GRACE"

But it is proper to God's honourable majesty so to be contemplated by his creatures . . . because of their much greater joy endlessly marvelling at the greatness of God, the Creator, and at the smallest part of all that is created.

For the contemplation of this makes the creature marvelously meek and mild; and therefore God wants us, and it is also proper to us, both by nature and by grace, to want to have knowledge of this, desiring the vision and the action. For it leads us in the right way, and keeps us in true life, and unites us to God. (LT, 327)

Selah

Julian calls us to contemplate God's majesty. Contemplation honors God, awakens us to the world we live in, and makes us sensitive to the "smallest part" of God's good world. Though most of us would not choose or could not choose the life of an enclosed contemplative, we all can learn much from Julian. There are at least three areas in which she can stimulate us to deepen our prayer life: (1) making use of visual images, (2) praying through hard questions, and (3) keeping a prayer journal. Julian blends wrestling with hard questions, such as understanding the nature of God and man or incarnation and atonement, with her visions or pictures of God.

MEDITATING ON
HOLY PICTURES

The Eastern Church has long venerated icons and perhaps done its best theology in these holy pictures. Pictures provide an immediacy found nowhere else. Icons give us a wonderful way to feel the hidden glory of the human Jesus ready to break out at any moment. In that strange stylized art, reverence is paid to his humanity and divinity. Icons of madonna and child display the touching sight of caring mother and small child, and usually suggest a level of hidden meaning. The mother is wistful, pondering the history about to unfold. The child is often regal, sitting upright and ready to give a blessing.

A few years ago in Hong Kong I led a retreat where I used some pictures as guides to meditation and prayer. One picture, created by Grunewald, was of the crucified Jesus. It was hung over the high altar at Isenheim in the seventeenth century and still has enormous pulling power. It shows Jesus emaciated and covered with running sores. I mentioned that it was intended to give comfort to us all, as we could see that Jesus identified with our pain, even sharing the most dreaded diseases. A missionary doctor was moved to use the picture in his private devotions to help serve people who were afflicted with terrible diseases that covered the body with sores.

Another time, while leading a prayer group of Chinese women, I used pictures taken from a *National Geographic* magazine featuring the women of China. These pictures made intercession more vivid for all present.

Julian's book is usually referred to as sixteen showings of love. Some of the revelations are very graphic, depicting the suffering of Jesus. Others are more intellectualized, symbolizing lessons given by a teaching Jesus. The book contains four graphic visions of the bleeding Christ. Julian is not squeamish about the subject, but is eager to see and search for meaning. The first revelation is of Christ who bled copiously. Accompanying this image, Julian saw Mary as a vulnerable adolescent, a model contemplative as she pondered the wonder that God would use her—a simple creature—to give birth to His son.

In the other three visions Julian is sensitive to color changes in the flesh of Christ. His dry skin turns to shades of blue and then to brown. In the vision of the second revelation, she has a strange experience of being taken to the ocean floor. She has no fear, for the crucified Christ accompanies her, no matter to what depths she is plunged. What a wonderful image and comfort for us in our prayer life!

In the vision of the fourth revelation, the blood flows in unending streams, filling all the universe. She thinks of this as spiritual water. We can drink of Christ's blood in communion to nourish our souls. We are baptized with holy water, which points to the cleansing blood of Christ, the real purifier. In the vision of the eighth revelation, Julian thinks of the words of Christ on the cross: "I thirst." She ponders the spiritual thirst of Christ.

Long ago I discovered that so-called realistic pictures of Christ did not help me in my devotional life. Sentimentality is almost always present, a reducing of Christ to emotions too easily provoked and too easily dismissed. Because Christ generates so many levels of meaning and his sacrifice was truly terrible, we need artists to give us several ways to visualize who he is. Who can express for us the fantastic, the awesome, the complex in limited human form?

I have found help in some surreal art and in icons from the Eastern Church. Dali, my favorite surreal artist, painted a picture I have long enjoyed. It is of the crucified Christ, inspired by reading Saint John of the Cross. The very white body of Christ on a cross, shown high in the picture and surrounded by a deep blackness, contrasts to the deep blue of the Sea of Galilee and the fisherman's boat in the bottom portion of the picture. It makes me feel connected to Julian's vision of the crucified Christ, filling the universe while still linked to his earthly experience.

Good religious art is complementary to religious texts. To the imaginative, seeking eye, anything can serve as visual stimulus to pray.

Lectio Divina

The Lord is my shepherd, I shall not want. He makes me lie down in green pastures; he leads me beside still waters; he restores my soul. He leads me in right paths for his name's sake. Even though

I walk through the darkest valley, I fear no evil; for you are with me; your rod and your staff—they comfort me. You prepare a table before me in the presence of my enemies; you anoint my head with oil; my cup overflows. Surely goodness and mercy shall follow me all the days of my life, and I shall dwell in the house of the Lord my whole life long. (Ps 23)

Examen

In the vision of her second revelation, Julian saw the bottom of the sea, covered with green hills, valleys, and moss strewn with seaweed and gravel. She could move about freely in this underworld, for the crucified Lord enabled her to experience life in any depth.

As you center yourself in silence before the Lord, imagine yourself in a peaceful, deep place. Move around the area freely, if you wish. Let the Lord come to you and ask you this question: What is the gift you desire from me?

Closing Meditation

Within all of Julian's pictures and thought, the crucified Jesus is central. Sensing that any departure from love ultimately expressed in the cross is dangerous, she remarked,

> *At this time I wanted to look away from the cross, but I did not dare, for I knew well that whilst I contemplated the cross I was secure and safe. Therefore I would not agree to put my soul in danger, for apart from the cross there was no safety from the fear of devils. So was I taught to choose Jesus for my heaven. . . . And this has always been a comfort to me, that I choose Jesus by his grace to be my heaven in all this time of suffering and of sorrow. (LT, 211-12)*

PRAYING THROUGH HARD QUESTIONS

Julian portrays the model of a good, integrated prayer life. She moves back and forth from image to conceptualization, from obvious doctrinal teaching to exploring its unobvious implications. She has a center, a focus on God as love. This defines for her the nature of God and man. While God is perfect lover, we are by nature also lovers, though we are imperfect.

In pursuing her lifelong wonder with the divine love, Julian develops a rich theology of God who has perfect fathering and mothering grace. Her thought is both simple and complex. Simply put, God is love at its fullest. Expression of this concept is complex, for God is our brother Jesus who is like a mother, a perfect warrior knight who knows no wrath, a triune God who moves out to create a single but varied community.

Julian wrestles with the basic teaching of her church that we are sinners worthy of condemnation, and also with her own experience that she does not want to displease God and feels no displeasure on His part. She eventually produces an original consoling treatment of no wrath in God, but she still fears the onslaught of devils who long for her damnation. She struggles with medieval pictures of punishment and hell and her own dominating pictures of a kindly Lord and His heaven. She eventually struggles with all major doctrines of her church.

A substantial prayer life surely deals with basic themes of theology: creation, fall, and redemption. How unfortunate that we relegate this to textbooks! We struggle to understand God and ourselves. God is both within our world and outside of it. We are like God and not like God. We sense that our lives are related to a hidden depth, and we long to understand who we really are.

Julian gives practical advice on how to grow in understanding. We integrate our resources. We are given three aids to living a life of meaning:

The first is the use of man's natural reason. The second is the common teaching of Holy Church. The third is the inward grace-giving operation of the Holy Spirit; and these three are all from one God. God is the foundation of our natural reason; and God is the teaching of Holy Church, and God is the Holy Spirit, and they are all different gifts, and he wants us to have regard for them, and to accord ourselves to them. (LT, 335)

A sure way to deepen our prayer life is to blend theological study with a personal passion to find workable attitudes and approaches to hard questions. Theological probing is not to be seen as the province of specialists; all who hunger for God thirst for understanding of God. We all have those moments when we ask, "Why?" Why is there a world? Why am I in it? Why am I yearning for that which I cannot name? Why can I not give up the cry for justice?

Lectio Divina

Who will separate us from the love of Christ? Will hardship, or distress, or persecution, or famine, or nakedness, or peril, or sword? . . . No, in all these things we are more than conquerors through him who loved us. For I am convinced that neither death, nor life, nor angels, nor rulers, nor things present, nor things to come, nor powers, nor height, nor depth, nor anything else in all creation, will be able to separate us from the love of God in Christ Jesus our Lord. (Rom 8:35, 37-39)

Examen

Consider these questions: What is the Lord's meaning to me? Can I trust God's love to be powerful enough to weave patterns of meaning throughout hard questions and harder circumstances?

Ask the Lord for the gift you desire.

Closing Meditation

And from the time that it was revealed, I desired many times to know what was our Lord's meaning. . . . So I was taught that love

48

is our Lord's meaning. . . . And in this love he has done all his works, and in this love he has made all things profitable to us, and in this love our life is everlasting. (LT, 342)

KEEPING A
PRAYER JOURNAL

Keeping a prayer journal is a valuable discipline. We have a way to chart our growth. Most of us find a strange spiraling at work. Questions and images that gripped us long ago return again and again, but there is never exact duplication in our pilgrimage.

Journal writing also helps us to articulate the struggle to think and pray. Like Julian, I have found hard theological thinking and prayer to be so intertwined that I do not know when I pass from one to the other. Much of the material in Julian, while in the form of report or analysis, can easily be lifted out and used as prayers throughout the day.

We all can be encouraged by reading accounts of how other Christians have coped with life. Devotional classics may not seem at first to be prayer journals, but often they are. Augustine's *Confessions* are a marvelous blend of autobiographical detail and theological probing. His thought moves naturally from question to prayer. He and Julian are akin.

I think everyone can be helped by keeping some kind of prayer or theological journal. The records may even be of value to others in the future. A caution must be registered, however. If we write with the feeling that someone is looking over our shoulder, or if we are trying to strike a good pious tone, we are defeated. We must honestly register failure and success, growth and stagnation.

Your journal should reflect your own individuality. Feel free to experiment. I often write summaries and excerpts from books I read. I sometimes write out prayers I wish to articulate and write down prayers I have discovered from others. Experiences of the day, dramatic and non-dramatic, may have pointed to an awareness of God at work.

Experiences of the night, time spent with family and dreams arising from the deeps, may point to other revelations or showings of love.

Almost nothing is known of Julian, not even her real name. But we can thank God that she has left record of her pilgrimage, her struggle, and her fresh discoveries of God. She invites us to think hard, agonize for prayerful integration of all our experiences, and articulate the journey.

A final quotation from Julian challenges us to so grow in prayer that we become partners in God's work. In this, we acknowledge the priority of God. God first loves us and moves us to love. God takes delight in our partnership, "much beholden to us for each good deed," but God is the ground of all love's possibilities. Such balance! Our love, prayer, and work count; but God is the source and facilitator of all.

Lectio Divina

One thing I asked of the Lord, that will I seek after: to dwell in the house of the Lord all the days of my life, to behold the beauty of the Lord, and to inquire in his temple. . . . I believe that I shall see the goodness of the Lord in the land of the living. Wait for the Lord; be strong, and let your heart take courage; wait for the Lord! (Ps 27:4, 13-14)

Examen

The stories of biblical characters are remembered and recorded. Julian's story is written down as well. Have you thought of a way you can articulate and remember your story?

Ask the Lord for the gift you desire.

Closing Meditation

O Love that wilt not let me go,
I rest my weary soul in thee;
I give thee back the life I owe,
That in thine ocean depths its flow
May richer, fuller be.
O Light that followest all my way,
I yield my flick'ring torch to thee;
My heart restores its borrowed ray,
That in thy sunshine's glow its day
May brighter, fairer be.

O Joy that seekest me through pain,
I cannot close my heart to thee;
I trace the rainbow thro' the rain,
And feel the promise is not vain
That morn shall tearless be.

O Cross that liftest up my head,
I dare not ask to hide from thee;
I lay in dust life's glory dead,
And from the ground there blossoms red
Life that shall endless be.
Amen.

FRANCIS OF ASSISI

❧ 1 ❧

CALLED TO
RADICAL DISCIPLESHIP

THE RICH YOUNG MAN

*May the fiery and honey-sweet power of your love, O Lord, wean
me from all things under heaven, so that I may die for love of your
love, who deigned to die for love of my love.*[1]

Selah

Francis was born into a wealthy family, although he later chose a life
of radical poverty or simplicity as a way to emulate his Lord.[2] His
father, who was a very successful cloth merchant, had great ambitions
for his son. While Francis would one day be expected to join his father
in expanding the family fortune, he had the privileges of a cushioned,
carefree youth. He was encouraged by his father and nurtured by a
doting mother who particularly loved Francis, the firstborn.

Francis grew up in the beautiful Umbrian hilltop town of Assisi,
surrounded by fields of sunflowers and silver-green olive trees. He
not only lived a privileged life by receiving an education, but he
enjoyed leisure time, which he used exploring and daydreaming in
the countryside of Assisi.

Francis received a basic Christian catechism with the medieval
flavor of hearing many wonder stories of martyrs and saints. He
attended the parish church of San Nicolo, next to his home, and
would have had ample opportunity to go to the cathedral, San Rufino.
Medieval churches filled with visual images, particularly of the crucified Jesus, would have been imprinted on his mind. In time, Francis
would believe he saw and heard the crucified Lord commissioning him
for special ministry. This Christ would call for a radical obedience.

Who was this strange man from medieval Italy who shook the church and still fascinates us today? For me, he is a fresh incarnation of the Incarnation, a living icon who makes it possible to see the Christ. He heard a call from his Lord to radical discipleship. For him, the key to absolute obedience was poverty, the stripping away of all things superfluous and unimportant. He rejected the wealth of the world so that he could gain the riches of a vital relationship with God.

We read in the Scriptures where Jesus warned a rich young man to be careful of losing his soul.

> If you wish to be perfect, go, sell your possessions, and give the money to the poor, and you will have treasure in heaven; then come, follow me. (Matt 19:21)

The rich youth turned away from Jesus in sadness, for he would not give up his great wealth. Francis heard a similar call, but he obeyed and discovered a profoundly rich relationship with God that has reached out to bless us all.

Lectio Divina

> *It is easier for a camel to go through the eye of a needle than for someone who is rich to enter the kingdom of God. (Luke 18:25)*

Examen

Is there anything in your life to which you cling so fiercely that it becomes an impediment to giving God absolute allegiance? Wealth in itself is not evil; it can do great good. But when does something become an obsession, a God substitute? Can you eventually let go of all things if necessary and finally let God be all in all?

Closing Meditation

> *The bishop of Assisi once said to Saint Francis: "I think your life is too hard, too rough. You don't possess anything in this world." And Francis replied, "My Lord, if we had possessions, we would need weapons to defend them." (Legend of Perugia, 17)*[3]

A PAINFUL CONVERSION

Most High, Glorious God, enlighten the darkness of my heart, and give me correct faith, sure hope and perfect charity, with understanding and knowledge, Lord, so that I may fulfill your holy and true command. Amen.[4]

Selah

Like most of us, Francis did not understand his mission in life all at once. He went through a process of conversion. We can trace some of the steps in that fascinating transformation of the soul. During his youth he was given a basic catechism and a world of rich visual images, which provided raw material for later patterns of understanding. Radical, conscious conversion to the speaking Christ, however, began in crisis experiences.

When Francis was a high-spirited youth of age twenty, he went to war. His city was fighting with the neighboring Perugia. His father was able to provide him a handsome outfitting allowance. The war, however, did not provide any glory for Francis or Assisi. Many of the youth of Assisi were slaughtered, and some were thrown into prison. Sons of the nobility and the rich were spared because their fathers could pay large ransoms.

Francis was not the son of a nobleman, but he was the son of a rich man. So his life was spared, but not before he lay in prison for about a year. Circumstances were harsh, and Francis possibly suffered from the effects of that imprisonment for the rest of his life. He endured not only physical suffering, but doubtlessly began to rethink where true glory lay.

He belonged to an age of chivalry and crusades. Knights in shining armor were to use their power for high causes of honor and justice. But in his first high cause, he had to face the barbarism of war. Two years later, in 1204, Francis tried again his fortunes as a noble warrior. An illustrious knight, Gautier de Brienne, decided to take southern Italy with the blessings of the pope. Again Francis was handsomely outfitted by his father. He got as far as Spoleto. He believed

God was directing him to give up the quest and return home. Returning home was an exercise of humiliation. Family and friends wondered what was troubling the indecisive youth. He was seeking some further word from God.

In 1205, Francis received a word from Christ. As he prayed in a deserted church, San Damiano on the edge of Assisi, he focused on a large crucifix still standing over the altar. The large Byzantine image mesmerized him. The suffering Christ had outstretched hands and eyes that seemed to look away into another dimension. Finally the image spoke: "Francis, repair my house." For Francis, the meaning seemed obvious. This church lay in ruins, and so did others in the area. Francis and his followers rebuilt three churches before he began to understand that the rebuilding of the church was to be more than physical renovation of structures.

Francis was on a new road. Two additional experiences deepened his conversion and thrust him into the radical new obedience he chose. Once, when on the outskirts of Assisi, he heard the clanging bells of a leper approaching. Lepers were required to keep their distance from others and to make it known when they were moving about in an area. Like all of us, Francis would have been repulsed by the sight of a face eaten away, but he felt compelled to act as Christ would act—with compassion.

He kissed the leper and was freed. He was liberated from an instinctive, self-protecting urge that would have excluded another soul from being loved and honored. It was an extreme testing of caring and going beyond the conventional limits of propriety, but all of his life had this radical quality.

Francis eventually had to confront his father and defy his will. It was a dramatic choice: Francis could obey God or his earthly father, but he could not do both. He finally had to tell his father about his choice of evangelical poverty. His father had become enraged when he discovered that his son had taken bolts of valuable material to a neighboring city, sold them quickly for cash, and planned to use the money for God. (He planned to rebuild churches and feed the poor with other people's money.)

The boy threw money away, and it wasn't even his! The father could not understand his son's strange behavior and insisted on his rights as father and proprietor. He appealed to the city magistrates to summon Francis and force him to restore what he had taken. He was instructed to take his case to the bishop and his court.

Standing before the bishop, Francis's father demanded a return of all that was his. Francis stripped himself naked, declaring that he gave back to his father all he had that came from him. Henceforth, he had only one father: his heavenly father. The gesture was powerful. The claims of the world through the earthly father were rejected. The claims of the emptied Christ to follow him were honored.

At first, many citizens of Assisi thought Francis had become a madman. While many jeered, some were watching and found themselves wondering if the madman could help them meet their hunger for God. Within two years after the trial, Francis had gathered a little band of disciples. He did not recruit them, and he did not repulse them. He became a focus for those persons hungering for God. It became obvious that Christ would live in this new holy community.

Francis, always inclined to interpret scriptures literally, remembered that Christ lived in community with a small group of disciples. His holy community went on preaching missions to lead people to repentance and to prepare the world for God's outpouring of power and gifts. Francis, of course, needed some minimal organization and plan. He sought the voice of God in scripture, giving preeminence to the Gospels.

In February of 1208, while worshiping at the Portiuncula, a chapel he had restored, Francis heard with a new apprehension the words being read for the service. They came from Matthew 10:7-10, a summons to mission:

> As you go, proclaim the good news, "The kingdom of heaven has come near." Cure the sick, raise the dead, cleanse the lepers, cast out demons. You received without payment; give without payment. Take no gold, or silver, or copper in your belts, no bag for your journey, or two tunics, or sandals, or a staff; for laborers deserve their food.

For Francis, God had spoken. He had the blueprint for his new organization. He still longed for confirmation or further instructions from God, so later he and some of the early disciples decided to seek more guidance from scripture. After attending a service, they asked the priest for permission to consult the Gospels. They let the Bible randomly fall open three times. In an uncanny way, the three texts corresponded to the Matthew texts that had so galvanized Francis. What were those three confirming texts?

> Take nothing for your journey, no staff, nor bag, nor bread, nor money—not even an extra tunic. (Luke 9:3)

> If any want to become my followers, let them deny themselves and take up their cross daily and follow me. (Luke 9:23)

> Sell all that you own and distribute the money to the poor, and you will have treasure in heaven; then come, follow me. (Luke 18:22)

Lectio Divina

> *Do not store up for yourselves treasures on earth, where moth and rust consume and where thieves break in and steal; but store up for yourselves treasures in heaven. . . . For where your treasure is, there your heart will be also. (Matt 6:19-21)*

Examen

Can you trace your conversion journey? You will keep turning more and more to the light as it appears, moving step by step. What events and persons moved you as you began turning toward God? Who and what deepens your conversion? Ask the Lord for the gift you desire.

Closing Meditation

> *The Lord has called me into the way of simplicity and humility, and he has indeed made this way known through me and through all who choose to believe me and follow me. . . . He told me that I am to be a new kind of fool in this world. (Mirror of Perfection, 68)[5]*

GROUNDING THE VISION

And after the Lord gave me some brothers, no one showed me what to do; but the Most High revealed to me that I was to live according to the manner of the Holy Ghost. And I had it written down in brief, simple words, and the Lord Pope confirmed it for me. And those who came to receive this life gave everything they had to the poor, and they were happy with one tunic patched, inside and out, and with a cord and breeches. And we had no desire for anything else. (The Testament of St. Francis)[6]

Selah

Francis believed God had spoken through scriptures, but he would check his private interpretation with mother church. He lived in an age in which the church was sensitive to heretical divisions, and he had no desire to splinter the church or deviate from its basic teachings. He sought approval from the pope. It is an interesting study in contrasts to put Francis beside Pope Innocent III. The pope was from a powerful aristocratic family and saw himself as the legitimate prince of power. He shook thrones and terrorized the disobedient.

Many persons know of the story about the pope having a dream of an endangered church. It would be saved by a humble son of the church. While we cannot know all that was in the mind of the pope, we can rejoice that he gave spoken permission for Francis to follow the simple rule he had presented. Official permission would come later, after revisions.

The Rule of the Friars Minor is a simple compilation of Gospel sayings and general principles. As long as the group was small, the charismatic personality of Francis substituted for the lack of specific regulations that would appear later. In the opening we find reference to the Gospel texts that had so gripped him:

> The rule and life of these brothers is this: to live in obedience, in chastity, and without anything of their own, and to follow the teaching and the footprints of our Lord Jesus Christ, who says "If you wish to be perfect, go and sell everything and give it to the poor, and

you will have treasure in heaven." Again, "if anyone wishes to come after me, let him deny himself and take up his cross and follow me." Again, "if anyone wishes to come to me and does not hate father and mother and wife and children and brothers and sisters, and even his own life, he cannot be my disciple."[7]

Francis did not intentionally aim at reforming the church, but did so. He could never have lived in defiance of the church as a schismatic. He believed that God was revealed in the God-Man, Jesus the Christ, and that this Christ was known in scripture and in the church's interpretation of scripture. His struggle for integrity had to be within the context of his mother church. In his struggle, the church was forced to struggle—with the Christ who always challenges his people accommodated too much to the power and glory of the world.

Lectio Divina

Let us love one another, because love is from God; everyone who loves is born of God and knows God. Beloved, since God loved us so much, we also ought to love one another. (1 John 4:7, 11)

Examen

Do you strive to use your private experience with God to bless the larger Christian family? It is so easy to withdraw and enjoy the sweetness of a private relationship with God. Are you willing to accept the hardships and challenges that come when you share your experience and mandates from God?

Closing Meditation

St. Francis said, "Because I haven't much strength to talk, tormented as I am with the pain of my illness, I shall make three brief statements of my will concerning the brothers. In memory of the blessing and testament I leave them, they should always love and respect one another; they should always love and be faithful to our lady Holy Poverty; and they should always be loyal subjects of the prelates and priests of Holy Mother Church. (Legend of Perugia, 62)[8]

Notes

[1]Attributed to Francis by Bernardine of Siena, quoted by Murray Bodo, *Through the Year with Francis of Assisi: Daily Meditations from His Words and Life* (New York: Image Books of Doubleday, 1987) 60.

[2]For a summary of the life of Francis, I prefer the following sources: Julien Green, *God's Fool: The Life and Times of Francis of Assisi* (London: Hodder & Stoughton, 1986); John Moorman, *St. Francis of Assisi* (London: SPCK, 1963); Duane Arnold and George Fry, *Francis: A Call to Conversion* (London: SPCK, 1988).

[3]Bodo, 49.

[4]Prayer of Francis before the Damiano Crucifix, Ibid., 57.

[5]Bodo, 23.

[6]Ibid., 38.

[7]"The Rule of the Friars Minor," *Francis and Clare: The Complete Works, The Classics of Western Spirituality* (New York: Paulist, 1982) 109.

[8]Bodo, 194.

∽2∽

PRAYER AS ADORATION

*I shall give You thanks, O Lord, most Holy Father, King of heaven
and earth, because you have consoled me. You are God my Savior;
I will be full of confidence and without fear. My strength and
my song is the Lord, and He has become my salvation.[1]*

Selah

Francis composed this psalm for matin, the first prayer time of the
day. It reveals adoration as his basic mode of communing with
God. He teaches us not to barge into the presence of God with our
agendas. While it is good to speak to God throughout the day, often in
natural short sentences, there must be those occasions when we take
time to be still in God's presence.

No matter how familiar we become with prayer forms, we should
constantly remind ourselves that prayer is related to a profound mystery: we humans can connect to a reality we cannot totally understand.
We must pause often to reflect on this wonder; God is beyond our
taming and even our conceiving, but God somehow connects to us.
We are loved and called to fellowship with God, which pulls from us
all we can give.

Francis was a man of constant prayer. He observed Holy Office, a
liturgical daily calendar of set prayers and scripture readings. In addi-
tion to the established routine of praying, he often withdrew for long
periods of meditation. He had a rhythm of using free prayers spoken
spontaneously and liturgical prayers that were done with the brothers.

Some of his prayers are full of beautiful images and rich thoughts,
as he had the spirit of a medieval troubadour. His imagination was rich
as he prayed of Brother Sun, Sister Moon, Lady Poverty, and others.
Some of his prayers were simple words or phrases repeated over and

over again in a sense of wonder, for example, the prayer of adoration "My God, My God."

In reflecting on the life of Francis, we notice how christocentric he was. His faith was not a Platonic gathering of concepts. He read the Gospels continuously and took quite literally the commands of Jesus. He envisioned the life of Jesus and celebrated each episode of the earthly savior. He adored the human Jesus, who was his brother as well as the Son of God. Of course, he related to the father God, the focus of Jesus' own prayers. His prayers to the Creator God reveal unusual sensitivity to the world of the Creator.

ADORING THE HUMAN JESUS

Francis was intimately united with Jesus—Jesus always in his heart, Jesus on his lips, Jesus in his ears, Jesus in his eyes, Jesus in his hands, Jesus in all the other members of his body. . . . Often when he was on a journey, meditating or singing about Jesus, he would leave the road and start inviting all creatures to praise Jesus. (Celano, First Life, 115)[2]

Selah

Francis had the deepest reverence for the humanity of Jesus. His devotion included probing the mystery of the infant Jesus, the adult Jesus, and the crucified Lord. He is usually given credit for constructing the first Christmas nativity creche in Greccio for midnight mass in 1223. According to the report, Francis invited a friend, John by name, to make a creche:

> For I wish to recreate the birth of the Babe born in Bethlehem, so that we will see with our own eyes how he did not even have the barest necessities, how he lay in a manger, how with an ox and an ass standing by, he lay upon the hay where he had been placed.[3]

People from the neighborhood came, dressed in festive costumes and carrying candles and torches. A manger was filled with hay, and an ox and an ass were led to stand by the manger-crib. Everyone was filled with delight; Francis was particularly filled with joy to see the Christ represented in such honor. Celano, the reporter, gave an interpretation that perfectly describes the mind of Francis:

> Then was gospel simplicity resplendent, poverty exalted, humility commended, and Greccio, as it were, a new Bethlehem. . . . The saint of God stood ecstatically before the manger, his spirit trembling with compassion and ineffable love. Then the priest celebrated the solemnity of the Eucharist over the manger, and he too experienced a consolation he'd never tasted before.[4]

Celano commented on the remarks Francis made at that memorable Christmas Eve mass. He spoke of the poor vulnerable King Jesus and about the little humble town of Bethlehem. Everyone was ravished with heavenly desire, for many people had not reflected on God come to us as the poor "Little Babe of Bethlehem."

When we pray, focused on the Lord Jesus, most of us envision a strong adult male. Pictures of Madonna and Child might remind us that the Christ went through all of the stages of life we have undergone. It would be good to view a picture of the Christ child sometimes and thank God that His Son experienced the vulnerability of infancy, the needs of a child, and the growing pains of leaving home and launching into a proper vocation.

Francis not only celebrated the love of God made incarnate in a vulnerable babe, he also celebrated and tried to imitate the loving work of the adult Jesus. If Jesus were celibate, poor, and an itinerant evangelist, so should Francis be. And he called his brothers to the same life. From the first days of the order, he sent his brothers out, two by two, to preach and teach. He literally followed the instruction of Jesus to his disciples, as found in Matthew 10.

Franciscan preachers performed a great ministry to an illiterate population. Few could buy books, and few could read. While the church touched everyone's life at crucial moments such as birth, marriage, and death, neither church nor society had enough schools to train the bulk of the population. People feasted on the pictorial presentation of the gospel in stained glass windows, carved wooden and stone sculptures, or paintings on mural walls. But with the coming of

Franciscan preachers into the villages and towns of Europe, people were given moving explanations of the gospel stories and commands. These preachers fed a people hungry for spiritual food.

It should not seem strange that people emptied the towns, wanting to follow the way of Francis. He again was forced to provide some kind of organization for devout laity. He wrote a Rule for a third order that made it possible for dedicated laypersons to observe some spiritual disciplines while still being responsible for their families and jobs. Some Protestants mistakenly label the vow of celibacy as impractical or unworthy.

Francis and his first order of brothers were celibate and thus free to move anyplace at anytime. Celibacy, like marriage, is a calling and a gift. Celibate Christians joined the first order of Francis or the second order established by Clare—women called to a life of intercessory prayer. The third order made a place for married persons. Francis, influenced by the monastic life of his day and a tendency to duplicate literally the life of Jesus, chose to be a celibate itinerant evangelist.

Using the words of Jesus in his Rule, Francis gave a way and expressed an attitude for his brothers to follow:

> When the brothers go about through the world, they should carry nothing for their journey, neither (Luke 9:3) a knapsack (Luke 10:4), nor a purse, nor bread, nor money (Luke 9:3), nor a staff (Matt 10:10). And into whatever house they enter, let them first say, "Peace to this house" (Luke 10:5). And remaining in that house, they may eat and drink whatever their hosts have offered (Luke 10:7). They should not offer resistance to evil (Matt 5:39), but if someone should strike them on one cheek, let them offer him the other as well. (Matt 5:39; Luke 6:29)[5]

We see how the Rule is simply a compiling of sayings from Jesus regarding the work his disciples were to do. Attention was paid to resistance and hostility. Francis, in his longing to imitate Jesus, considered martyrdom a high calling.

Francis gives guidance to those adults who pray for wisdom in choosing a vocation and knowing whether or not to marry. Some of us choose celibacy because the nature of our work and the shape of our personalities find this mode to be the best way to serve God. Some of us choose marriage and find the discipline of living with another a way to grow in love. We should pray for perseverance because we will encounter resistance and hostility in all vocations. Once we are committed to a work that we believe is pleasing to God, we speak to God often about the work, finding strength to accept the hardships and with them the strange joy God gives.

Francis then not only honored the work of the adult evangelist Jesus, but also his sacrifice. He spent much time meditating on the crucified Lord. We recall his dramatic moment of commissioning when he believed Christ spoke to him through the old Byzantine crucifix hanging in San Damiano. As he grew older, he thought more and more about the crucifixion. We have this remark from *The Little Flowers of St. Francis:*

> He wanted somehow to suffer with Jesus, and so, two years before he died, this prayer rose from the depths of his love for the crucified Lord: "O Lord, I beg of you two graces before I die: to experience personally and in all possible fullness the pain of your bitter passion, and to feel for you the same love that moved you to sacrifice yourself for us."[6]

In 1224, shortly before his death, while meditating alone on Mount Alverna, Francis received the gift of the stigmata. The stigmata is a phenomenon dear to many Catholic hearts and incomprehensible to many Protestants. The stigmata are five wounds borne by a person in the two hands, two feet, and side, corresponding to the five wounds of the crucified Jesus. Some devout Christians so identify with the crucified Jesus that they come to share his suffering literally.

Obviously the Catholic church has felt the need to speak carefully of this matter. Raphael Brown, a third order Franciscan and editor of an edition of *The Little Flowers,* is a good representative voice. He acknowledges that some people, who are not necessarily religious, evince signs of body abnormality in critical situations. Mothers have performed superhuman feats when their children were in danger. People identifying with disabled persons may develop body symptoms like those of the ones they love. Though some cases may seem explainable, others are not. There is room for belief that sometimes God miraculously grants the stigmata to a chosen saint.[7] This issue, of course, would not be so open to doubt in the medieval period, and, by the way, is not necessarily a negative judgment on the faith of an earlier generation.

There was soon published along with *The Little Flowers* a work called *The Considerations on the Holy Stigmata*. It was a series of five meditations, corresponding to the five wounds received by Jesus, then by Francis. The third consideration discusses the vision Francis received of the crucified Lord at the time he received the stigmata:

> And the fervor of his devotion increased so much within him that he utterly transformed himself into Jesus through love and compassion. And while he was thus inflaming himself in this contemplation, on that same morning he saw coming down from heaven a Seraph with six resplendent and flaming wings. As the Seraph, flying swiftly, came closer to Saint Francis, so that he could perceive him clearly, he noticed that he had the likeness of a Crucified Man and his wings were so disposed that two wings extended above his head, two were spread out to fly, and the other two covered his entire body.[8]

This is a strange fused picture. Seraphs belong to the celestial realm, their very form signifying the terrifying, beautiful power of God in divine otherness, God's distance from the everyday world of men. But the fiery creature embraced the human Jesus, caught up to God.

Perhaps the best way to evaluate the worth of unusual visions or experiences is to see how they connect to the will and lives of those affected. Francis longed with all his heart to walk in the steps of Jesus, to make his life a model for his own. His intentions and prayers issued forth in a remarkable life of love and service. His visions point to the awesome, unspeakable glory of God.

Francis reminds us constantly that the awesome sovereign God of the universe is revealed in His suffering Son and suffering disciples of His Son. Our prayer life, if it has the intimacy with God enjoyed by Francis, does not shrink from thinking on the pain of love. Suffering is not accepted for its own sake, but as a means to understand what God felt in the death of Christ and as a sign that our work and love for God will surely bear fruit.

Lectio Divina

When Mary came where Jesus was and saw him, she knelt at his feet and said to him, "Lord, if you had been here, my brother would not have died." When Jesus saw her weeping, and the Jews who came with her also weeping, he was greatly disturbed in spirit and deeply moved. He said, "Where have you laid him?" They said to him, "Lord, come and see." Jesus began to weep. (John 11:32-36)

Examen

We miss the fullness of God's outpouring in the human Jesus in at least two ways: We so emphasize the divine nature of Christ that we fail to understand his human struggles and joys, and many of us relate only to the adult Jesus.

Today, meditate on the delight that the infant Jesus brought to his parents. Think on the struggle of Jesus to understand his mission and then to embrace it.

Closing Meditation

We are his spouses when our faithful souls are wed to Jesus Christ by the Holy Spirit. We are his brothers and sisters when we do the will of his Father who is in heaven. (Letter of Francis to All the Faithful)9

ADORING THE CREATOR GOD

Let us adore God with pure hearts because we need to pray con-
tinually and never lose heart, for the Father seeks such worshipers.
God is Spirit, and those who worship him must worship in spirit
and truth. (Franciscan Rule of 1221)[10]

Selah

Because Francis was so christocentric, he did not neglect worship of the father God, the focus of the prayer life of Jesus. In his rich worship life he submitted to the discipline of Holy Office. This set liturgical timetable for daily worship was unusually full of references to the Psalms, which celebrated the rule of a good and just sovereign God. Francis added special scriptures to be read along with the seven prescribed times of prayer each day.

Many people gifted with the desire and discipline for liturgical prayer have been blessed by Francis who infused old forms with freshness. In his little book on Francis, Carlo Carretto offers a Holy Office he composed, using prayers from Francis and psalms that Francis would have used for the seven prayer times. He suggests that we observe Holy Office in some way.[11]

We do not have to set aside seven times a day for prayer. In fact, many monastics have combined the offices into fewer prayer times. Four times for prayer—morning, noon, early evening, and before bed—are not too hard to manage. Like Caretto, we should feel free to put together our own scheme. Consulting lectionaries and prayer guides are useful, but we should honor our unique temperament and style.

Carretto uses a "naming prayer" from Francis for one of his early devotions. It is one we can imitate and comes from a letter Francis wrote to his beloved Brother Leo:

You alone are holy, Lord God, Worker of Wonders.
You are strong.
You are great.
You are the Most High.
You are omnipotent, our holy Father,
> King of heaven and earth.
You, Lord God, one and three,
> are our every good.
You, Lord God, all good, our highest good—
> Lord God living and true.
You are charity and love.
You are wisdom.
You are humility.
You are patience.
You are safety.
You are peace.
You are joy and happiness.
You are justice and temperance.
You are the fullness of riches.
You are beauty.
You are gentleness.
You are our protector.
You are our keeper and defender.
You are our strength.
You are our refreshment.
You are our hope.
You are our faith.
You are our great sweetness.
You are our eternal life, great and admirable Lord,
> Almighty God, merciful Savior.[12]

We cannot discuss the lyrical prayers of Francis to his Creator without mentioning his classic "Canticle of Brother Sun." Its various parts are from different time periods, but the ending section to Sister Death comes towards the end of the life of Francis. The prayer reveals the sensitivity of Francis to God's living world in all its specific unique forms, just as his devotion is to a personal God focused in the human unique Jesus.

PRAYING WITH THE SAINTS

Most High, all-powerful, good Lord,
    All praise be yours, all glory, all honour,
    And all blessing.

To you alone, Most High, do they belong.
    No mortal lips are worthy
    To pronounce your name.

All praise be yours, my Lord, with all your creatures,
    Especially Sir Brother Sun,
    Who brings the day; and light you give us through him.

How beautiful is he, how radiant in his splendour!
    Of You, Most High, he is the token.

All praise be yours, my Lord,
    for Sister Moon and the Stars;
    In the heavens you have made them, bright
    And precious and fair.

All praise be yours, my Lord,
    for Brother Wind, and the Air,
    and fair and stormy, all the weather's moods,
    By which you cherish all that you have made.

All praise be yours, My Lord, for Sister Water,
    so useful, lowly, precious, and pure.

All praise be yours, My Lord, for Brother Fire,
    Through whom you brighten the night.
    How beautiful is he, how gay, robust, and strong!

All praise be yours, My Lord,
    for Sister Earth, our mother,
    Who feeds us, rules us, and produces
    Various fruits with coloured flowers and herbs.

All praise be yours, My Lord, for those who forgive
    For love of you and endure
    Infirmity and tribulation.

Happy are those who endure them in peace,
>For by you, Most High, they will be crowned.

All praise be yours, My Lord, for Sister Physical Death,
>from whose embrace no mortal can escape.

Woe to those who die in mortal sin!
>Happy are those she finds doing your most holy will!
>The second death can do no harm to them.

Praise and bless my Lord, and give him thanks,
>And serve him with great humility.[13]

We have looked at beautiful articulated prayers, having that Christian troubadour flair that only Francis has. But he also observed periods of silence and had prayers of few words. We mentioned earlier the prayer he uttered all night when he was in the home of his first disciple, Bernard. In joyous focusing on the love of God, he could only say "My God, My God."

Scripture speaks of Jesus retiring from the public scene from time to time to meditate and pray to his father. Francis, imitator of Jesus that he was, would also incorporate large blocks of time for intense private devotion. He loved two mountain retreats in particular: Subasio and Alverna. High on these wooded hills, usually in a cave, Francis would withdraw for long periods of meditation. Each of us must find our own balance.

Lectio Divina

The heavens are telling the glory of God; and the firmament proclaims his handiwork. Day to day pours forth speech, and night to night declares knowledge. . . . Let the words of my mouth and the meditation of my heart be acceptable to you, O Lord, my rock and my redeemer. (Ps 19:1, 2, 14)

Examen

The Psalms, so familiar to Francis, give us all a prayer vocabulary. To commit some psalms to memory is to provide a reservoir in the soul. But sometimes we need to stop the flow of the many rich thoughts and words that can flood the mind. Like Francis, we need some times in which we use a single word or phrase. His famous prayer was the night-long cry: "My God, My God." Another word to still the mind and focus the heart may be: "Love, Love."

Closing Meditation

St. Francis praised the Artist in every one of his works; whatever he found in things made, he referred to their Maker. He rejoiced in all the works of the Lord's hands, and with joyful vision saw into the reason and cause that gave them life. In beautiful things he came to know Beauty itself. (Celano, Second Life, 165)[14]

Notes

[1] *The Writings of St. Francis of Assisi*, trans. Ignatius Brady (Assisi: Casa Editrice Francescana, C.E.F.A., 1989) 43.
[2] Ibid., 226.
[3] Murray Bodo, *Through the Year with Francis of Assisi: Daily Meditations from His Words and Life* (New York: Image Books of Doubleday, 1987) 230.
[4] Ibid., 231.
[5] "The Rule of the Friars Minor," *Francis and Clare: The Classics of Western Spirituality* (New York: Paulist, 1982) 120.
[6] Bodo, 187.
[7] *The Little Flowers of St. Francis*, trans. Raphael Brown (Garden City NJ: Image Books of Doubleday, 1958) 322-24.
[8] Ibid., 191.
[9] Bodo, 96.
[10] Ibid., 135.
[11] Carlo Carretto, *I, Francis* (London: William Collins, 1982) 137-38.
[12] Ibid., 139-40.
[13] *Francis and Clare*, 38-39.
[14] Bodo, 166.

𝕮𝕺3𝕺

PRAYER AS
INTERCESSION

Therefore take the whole armor of God, so that you may be able to withstand on that evil day, and having done everything, to stand firm. Stand therefore, and fasten the belt of truth around your waist, and put on the breastplate of righteousness. As shoes for your feet put on whatever will make you ready to proclaim the gospel of peace. With all of these, take the shield of faith, with which you will be able to quench all the flaming arrows of the evil one. Take the helmet of salvation, and the sword of the Spirit, which is the word of God. (Eph 6:13-17)

Selah

While Francis forsook the ideal of being a secular warrior, he did engage in spiritual battle on several fronts. His church literally took up arms, launching crusades or holy wars, against enemies within and without the church. Francis found another way to deal with the enemies of God. His intercessory prayers issued forth in campaigns of preaching and teaching. It would be useful to see how he became a part of the church's effort to restore heretics, enemies from within.

DEALING WITH THE ENEMY
WITHIN THE CHURCH

When it was evening, he took his place with the twelve; and while they were eating, he said, "Truly, I tell you, one of you will betray me." And they became greatly distressed and began to say to him one after another, "Surely not I, Lord?" (Matt 26:20-22)

Selah

During the lifetime of Francis, a heretical movement gained great strength in Christendom. These simple folk were called the Cathari, sometimes termed Albigensians.[1] They were dualists, believing that this world was created and governed by an evil power and the heavenly world was governed by a good power. Since this world in all material form was evil, Christ was not seen as having a real body or having gone through a real death. They rejected much of the Old Testament with its strong affirmation of this-worldly grace and focused on the Gospel of John, which seemed the most "spiritual" of all teachings.

In 1208, Pope Innocent III blessed a crusade aimed at destroying the Cathari. He blessed Simon de Montfort, an ambitious and ruthless man, who, in the name of God and the church, decimated the Cathari. What an interesting contrast to place Innocent III and Montfort against Francis! They were concerned about the unity of the church and purity of doctrine, but they were not the same kind of soul.

The Cathari were people starved for religious instruction. Many clergy were inadequate for the job of teaching. The people were surely offended by unworthy churchmen who claimed to be spiritual but lived within a gross materialism. While Francis could not save the Cathari, he and his brothers made contact with others who were hungry for some fuller knowledge of the gospel. They would sometimes stop and help the peasants in their work. They preached a simple message in love and did not seek wealth and power from their work. They had their own special weapons fighting the enemy within the church.

The prayer of Francis to be useful to God pushed him outside enclosed monasteries and away from bishops' thrones. He teaches us to pray for wisdom to discern the enemies within the church. He identified the enemies: ignorance of the gospel, unworthy clergy, false doctrine that denied the goodness of God's beautiful but broken world. He teaches us to pray for a constantly cleansed church and good teachers who help us to celebrate the goodness of life here and now.

Lectio Divina

He said to him the third time, "Simon son of John, do you love me?" Peter felt hurt because he said to him the third time, "Do you love me?" And he said to him, "Lord, you know everything; you know that I love you." Jesus said to him, "Feed my sheep." (John 21:17)

Examen

What spiritual weapons do you use? It is naive to believe a perfect church can ever exist that will not experience periodic internal struggles. But do we dare believe that God will work through an imperfect church, including imperfect people such as ourselves?

Closing Meditation

Jesus Christ, our Lord, whose footsteps we're to follow, called his betrayer "friend" and willingly handed himself over to his crucifiers. Our friends, then, are all those who unjustly inflict upon us tests and ordeals, shame and injury, sorrows and torments, martyrdom and death. They are the ones we should love most, for what they're really inflicting upon us is eternal life. (Franciscan Rule of 1221)[2]

DEALING WITH THE ENEMY OUTSIDE THE CHURCH

You have heard that it was said, "You shall love your neighbor and hate your enemy." But I say to you, Love your enemies and pray for those who persecute you, so that you may be children of your Father in heaven. (Matt 5:43-45a)

Selah

I remember visiting San Rufino, the cathedral church of Assisi, and seeing a startling sculpture outside the church. It was of a lion devouring a Muslim. It was intended to encourage the faithful that God would overcome all heresy and evil. Most people in the medieval period believed holy wars were justified, even desired, by God. Whether Francis gave some credence to this view cannot be known, but we do know he chose another way to deal with the heretic outside the church. He longed to preach to the Muslims, and he saw martyrdom as a high prize to be won.

His early Rule contains a whole chapter dealing with "Of the Brothers Who Go among the Saracens and Other Infidels." Like the other chapters, it is a compilation of Gospel sayings that pertain to the subject at hand. The following is an excerpt from it:

> The Lord says, "Behold I send you as sheep in the midst of wolves. Be therefore wise as serpents and simple as doves" (Matt 10:16)....
>
> And all the brothers, wherever they are, must remember that they have given themselves and handed over their bodies to the Lord Jesus Christ. And for love of Him they must expose themselves to enemies both seen and unseen; for the Lord says, "Whoever shall lose his life for me will save it unto life eternal (Luke 9:24; Matt 25:46). Blessed are they who suffer persecution for justice' sake, for theirs is the kingdom of heaven (Matt 5:10). If they have persecuted me, they will also persecute you (John 15:20). . . .
>
> "And do not fear those who kill the body (Matt 10:8) and thereafter can do no more (Luke 12:4). See that you be not troubled (Matt 24:6), for in your patient endurance you shall possess your souls (Luke 21:19). And whoever holds out to the end will be saved" (Matt 10:22; 24:13).[3]

Francis tried three times to go to the land of the Moors and evangelize them. Each time he failed. Finally in 1219, he was successful in getting to Syria. From there he moved to Damietta, Egypt, the site of a great Crusader army preparing to go to war. Francis spent six months in the camp, becoming evangelist to both Christians and Muslims. Surely he remembered his youthful dreams of being a holy knight. Again he would find disillusionment with the knights he found.[4]

Prayer as Intercession

In August of 1219, Christians made an assault on Damietta and were defeated. Francis had begged them not to attack, but his caution was unheeded. They were goaded on to wipe out the enemy by the pope's legate. Retreating and gathering new strength, the Christians prepared for a new battle. The Muslims inside Damietta were besieged and weakened by lack of supplies.

In November of 1219, the Crusaders again attacked Damietta. This time they succeeded. Women were raped, children sold into slavery, and men slaughtered. Again Francis had to see the barbarism of war. The Muslims retired sixty miles south of Damietta and gathered new forces. The sultan promised a piece of gold for every Christian head presented to him. A terrible reckoning was at hand.

At this time Francis went into the enemy camp and asked for an audience with the sultan. The sultan listened courteously to the courageous holy man from the Christian camp. Francis presented his simple gospel message focused on the loving Jesus, incarnation of God, and means of salvation. He even made an offer to prove the truth of his message. He proposed that he and some Muslim holy men walk through fire; the one unhurt would be the one protected by God. The sultan declined the offer, but showed great respect for Francis.

What do we make of such a story? Francis did not end the crusade, and to some persons, his efforts would seem to be absolute madness. Again he took literally the words of Jesus as found in the Gospels. Did not Jesus say, "Blessed are the peacemakers for they shall be called the children of God?" Did not Jesus say, "Love your enemies; pray for your enemies"?

Though Francis did not stop that particular war, we still remember this story and pause to think on his "madness." We might come to believe that war is never a real or lasting solution. We might redefine "enemy" and perhaps struggle with the hard teachings of the Sermon on the Mount. Francis urges us into this difficult area of prayer: How do we resist a different point of view without demonizing the other party and losing sight of the fact that we all are beloved children of God? What are our proper weapons of spiritual warfare? What is our prayerful intent: humiliation of the foe or conversion of us all to God who is sovereign love?

Lectio Divina

Do not judge, so that you may not be judged. For with the judgment you make you will be judged, and the measure you give will be the measure you get. Why do you see the speck in your neighbor's eye, but do not notice the log in your own eye? (Matt 7:1-3)

Examen

Bring to light those persons whom you think are enemies of the common good, even of God. What is in their point of view or grievance that needs to be heard? Pray for the strength to not become so judgmental that hatred takes control and peacemaking becomes impossible.

Closing Meditation

The Lord says in the gospel, "Love your enemies . . . You do in fact love your enemy when you do not brood over the evil another has done to you, but grieve instead over the sin on the other's soul, while continuing to act with love for the love of God. (Admonition 9)[5]

THE CLASSIC PRAYER
OF INTERCESSION

Blessed are the peacemakers, for they will be called children of God. (Matt 5:9)

Selah

Without doubt, the prayer attributed to Francis to be an instrument of God's peace is timeless. Although it cannot be traced further back than the nineteenth century, it so reflects the spirit of Francis that it will always be associated with him. It has enabled Christians in every generation to move beyond preoccupation with self

82

to a healthy regard for others. It should be memorized and meditated upon frequently. We look again at this magnificent intercession:

> Lord, make me an instrument of your peace.
> Where there is hatred, let me sow love,
> where there is injury, pardon,
> where there is doubt, faith,
> where there is despair, hope,
> where there is darkness, light,
> where there is sadness, joy.
>
> O Divine Master, grant that I may
> not so much seek to be consoled, as to console,
> not so much to be understood, as to understand,
> not so much to be loved, as to love;
>
> for it is in giving that we receive,
> it is in pardoning that we are pardoned,
> it is in dying that we awake to eternal life.[6]

Perhaps a good way to reflect on this classic prayer is to examine how it enabled a twentieth-century Christian to be a peacemaker in a violent situation. Alan Paton, born in 1903 in South Africa, entered a world of total racial separation. Whites could not legally attend black churches in African townships without a government permit, and those permits were rarely given. Persons of the ruling white class were chiefly members of the Dutch Reformed Church and were taught they had a "civilizing mission" in Africa. They were to bring the fruits of Christian enlightenment, a higher culture, and this could not be done if the races were mixed.

In our most recent history, the seemingly impossible has happened. South Africa has not only dismantled its apartheid policy, but has even elected as leader of the nation a man imprisoned for twenty-seven years, Nelson Mandela. Reading his autobiography, *Long Walk to Freedom,* is a jolting experience, as we see how entrenched and blind the old system of apartheid was. The battle for a new order was a long one, and pressure came steadily from those moved by a Christian vision for justice.

Paton was one of those voices that courageously stood for change. He did not leave his country from disgust or fear. He stayed and fought. He did not see himself as a particularly strong man. What enabled him to defy a mammoth system so tightly locked in place? He discovered the prayer of Saint Francis, "Lord, make me an instrument of thy peace."

He meditated on this prayer for seventeen years and wrote a book inspired by the prayer, *Instrument of Thy Peace.* He claimed in his opening chapter that the spirit of Francis revived the spirit of Christ within him. This spiritual power dispelled his melancholy, ended his self-pity, and energized him to be active in compassion.

The following prayer demonstrates how closely Paton followed the spirit of Francis:

> Lord, teach me the meaning of your commandment to love our enemies, and help me to obey it. Make me the instrument of your love, which is not denied to the hungry, the sick, the prisoner, the enemy.
>
> Teach me to hate division, and not to seek after it. But teach me also to stand up for those things that I believe to be right, no matter what the consequences may be. And help me this day to do some work of peace for you, perhaps to one whom I had thought to be my enemy.[7]

In his prayer life, Francis neglected neither adoration nor intercession. This meant he made time to still himself in the presence of God. He did not identify God with his agendas, but he did not forget his brothers and sisters. He knew there was a time for involvement in the world and a time to withdraw, a time to surrender power and a time to exert power.

He interceded for his order and for his church, though he knew disappointment with both. He interceded for his better self, to have the Christlike attitude that could be stripped bare and be present for others. His power as example for peacemaker is always present. The experience of Alan Paton, energized by Francis, can be ours as well.

PRAYER AS INTERCESSION

Lectio Divina

Likewise the Spirit helps us in our weakness; for we do not know how to pray as we ought, but that very Spirit intercedes for us with sighs too deep for words. (Rom 8:26)

Examen

Think of peacemakers who have energized you to do the hard work of intercession. Peacemakers have to disrupt society from its complacency with injustice or callousness before real peace can come. Can you pray with a Martin Luther King, "Lord give me strength to love and not to hate"?

Closing Meditation

Be confident in making your needs known to one another. For each of you, to the extent that God gives you grace, should love and nourish one another as a mother loves and nourishes her child. (Franciscan Rule of 1221)[8]

Notes

[1]Kenneth Scott Latourette, *A History of Christianity* (New York: Harpers, 1953) 453-58.

[2]Murray Bodo, *Through the Year with Francis of Assisi: Daily Meditations from His Words and Life* (New York: Image Books of Doubleday, 1987) 64.

[3] *The Writings of St. Francis*, trans. Ignatius Brady (Assisi: Casa Editrice Francescana, C.E.F.A., 1989) 76-77.

[4]For a discussion of Francis's mission to the Muslims, see Julien Green, *God's Fool: The Life and Times of Francis of Assisi* (London: Hodder & Stoughton, 1986) 203-208; and Duane Arnold and George Frye, *Francis: A Call to Conversion* (London: SPCK, 1988) 53-57.

[5]Bodo, 121.

[6] *The Lion Book of Famous Prayers* (Oxford: Lion Publishing, 1983) 30.

[7]Alan Paton, *Instrument of Thy Peace* (New York: Seabury, 1983) 114.

[8]Bodo, 27.

ꙮ4ꙮ

PRAYER AS
SURRENDER

*Very truly, I tell you, unless a grain of wheat falls into the earth
and dies, it remains just a single grain; but if it dies, it bears much
fruit. Those who love their life lose it, and those who hate their life
in this world will keep it for eternal life. (John 12:24-25)*

Selah

In examining the prayer life of Francis, we notice how his prayers of
adoration and surrender are inextricable. One way we can probe
the struggle of Francis to achieve a prayerful attitude of surrender is
to use two rubrics. He worked at giving up power both in the world
and in the church. Secondly, he also worked to prepare for a good
death. He offers us a powerful warning to resist the subtle tempta-
tions of being captive to power lusts in the world and in the church.
He teaches us to put death in the larger perspective; Sister Death is not
to be feared but welcomed when her moment to embrace us has come.

GIVING UP POWER IN THE WORLD

*It is easier for a camel to go through the eye of a needle than for
someone who is rich to enter the kingdom of God. (Luke 18:25)*

Selah

Because Francis was born into a rich family as the eldest son, he had
great prospects for worldly success. We remember the dramatic
struggles of his youth as he gave up the worldly dream of being a shining knight in armor and the worldly dream of being a business success.
He was a failure as a secular warrior. His experience as a twenty-year-

old boy, ending in a year's captivity as a prisoner of war, set him thinking about another pathway to honor.

He was a failure as a businessman. He expressed no interest in promoting his father's business, but with impetuous zeal sold some of his father's choice garments to help rebuild mother church. When his father took him to the bishop's court, charging him with abuse of another's property and lack of filial obedience, Francis was given the opportunity to declare his convictions. He would choose God and God's choice servant Lady Poverty. He would beg for food and preach to people of a loving God who provided for those who were simple and trusting.

Another story is told in *The Little Flowers*. Francis once told Brother Ruffino to go to Assisi, strip himself naked, and preach to the people whatever God should inspire him to say.[1] Brother Ruffino was a contemplative who spoke very little. He had no great gift for preaching and did not feel the need for articulating his faith in words. He hesitated when commanded by Francis, pleading that he was not a man of eloquence. Francis reprimanded him for not obeying immediately and in complete faith that God would provide the words. He ordered the brother to go to Assisi "naked and clothed only in thy breeches" and to preach.

Brother Ruffino obeyed Francis. As he made his reverence to the altar and started to mount the pulpit stairs, the children and adults of Assisi began to laugh. They saw the matter as an exaggerated way to do penance and wondered about the lunacy of the brother. In the meanwhile, Francis thought about his rash command. Brother Ruffino was from a distinguished family, a good and gentle man who felt his lack of eloquence. Francis regretted his order and decided to join the brother, naked in the pulpit. As Francis entered the church, he too was greeted with laughter and pity.

Brother Ruffino had been exhorting the people to flee from the snares of the world lest they endanger their souls for eternal damnation. Francis joined the brother and continued the homily. He spoke of contempt for the world and joy for the kingdom of God. He pointed to the Son of God who was stripped naked and crucified. He spoke of the freedom of evangelical poverty and simple trust in a loving God of providence. By the time Francis had finished, the multitudes present were weeping with "wondrous devotion and contrition of heart." Brother Leo, who had accompanied Francis to the church, then produced the habits of the brothers. They reclothed themselves and returned to the Portiuncula, praising God.

This story has a childlike charm at one level, but it can be a valuable warning and rebuke at another level. Francis lived in a culture where ministers of the church wore beautiful robes and spoke in polished liturgical phrases not always understood by the people. And the people wore their finery to be seen by all and, like all of us regular churchgoers, were likely to duplicate the usual acts of worship without fresh engagement with God.

Francis literally stripped away all impediments to meeting God. We ministers must incorporate into our prayer life this concern not to separate ourselves from God and people by the externals of dress and language. We laity must pray for the courage to be stripped before God, to let God break into our lives repeatedly and not allow our ministers and God to be held back by any external forms of custom.

Another story dear to the heart of all Franciscans is "What Is Perfect Joy?" Though told in various forms, the following version is the one most scholars think is the original.[2] One day Francis summoned Brother Leo to come and write down the story that illustrated perfect joy. According to the story, a messenger arrived to tell Francis that all the university masters at Paris had entered his order. But this was not true joy. Then he was told that bishops and archbishops, the king of France, and the king of England had entered his order. But this also was not true joy. He was told that his brothers had gone to the infidels, and all of them had been converted to the Christian faith. This was not true joy. He was given power to heal the sick and work many miracles. This was not true joy.

Francis returned from Perugia in the depths of winter and suffered the bitter chill of the cold. He knocked at the gates of the brothers' house and asked for admittance. He was told to go away, for it was not a decent hour to be going about. He knocked again and requested admission. He was told to go away, as he must be an idiot. He tried again to gain entry and pled for mercy in the name of God. He was rejected. The conclusion: "I tell you Leo if I would put up with all this and not be upset, in this is true joy and real virtue and the salvation of one's soul."

This story has an extreme edge, but there is exaggeration in much that pertains to Francis. Again he is teaching us not to be dazzled by what seem to be wonderful and worthy gifts. What Christian would not be pleased to see the conversion of unbelievers, to see the honoring of the gospel among intellectuals, to lead kings and the powerful of the earth to recognize their need for humility? What Christian would not be honored to have great gifts of preaching or healing?

For Francis, however, the priority of values is all-important. It is more important to have mastery of one's soul, an unshakable faith in God that can endure success or lack of success. To endure the ingratitude or lack of understanding from others is a small thing compared to being stayed on a thankful, trusting belief in the sovereignty of God.

Lectio Divina

Not that I am referring to being in need; for I have learned to be content with whatever I have. I know what it is to have little, and I know what it is to have plenty. In any and all circumstances I have learned the secret of being well-fed and of going hungry, of having plenty and of being in need. I can do all things through him who strengthens me. (Phil 4:11-13)

Examen

We need to do housecleaning frequently, clearing out the accumulated junk, the excesses. Can we see the surrender of things and power as a way to renew our first love of God? In the beginning of assuming our life's work, many of us had little; and yet we had what counted.

Closing Meditation

As far as the brothers distance themselves from poverty, that far will the world distance itself from the brothers, and they search and not find. But if they remain the embrace of my Lady Poverty, the world will nourish them, for then they are given the world for its salvation. (Celano, Second Life, 70)[3]

Giving up Power in the Church

But Jesus called them to him and said, "You know that the rulers of the Gentiles lord it over them, and their great ones are tyrants over them. It will not be so among you; but whoever wishes to be great among you must be your servant, and whoever wishes to be first among you must be your slave; just as the Son of Man came not to be served but to serve, and to give his life as a ransom for many." (Matt 20:25-28)

Selah

Francis also worked on giving up power in the church and within his own order. I find it remarkable that a man who had such high reverence for the Eucharist never sought ordination as a priest. He deeply revered the office of priests, for they had the permission and power of the church to offer up the body and blood of Christ for a worshiping community. But priests and bishops were people of power, and Francis preferred to serve Lady Poverty who did not crave power.

Changes that took place within his order must have been a great cross for Francis to have borne. The order had grown like wildfire, and new currents of thought arose that challenged his radical vision. Francis visited Bologna in 1220. The city was inordinately proud of its university, perhaps the oldest in Europe, certainly the seat of its finest law school. There he found Friars Minor, men of his own order, who continued to hold their prestigious academic positions and their homes.

They did not question the integrity of Francis, but they questioned his organization. They felt a need to relax the stringent requirements and certainly not maintain what seemed to be an anti-academic attitude towards faith. We recall that Francis did not approve of his brothers accumulating books and spending hours away from prayer in doing scholastic disputations. Again Lady Poverty was not a collector of precious books, nor did she gain satisfaction in winning scholarly contests.

Leaving Bologna, Francis went on to Orvieto. The new pope had appointed Cardinal Ugolino, who would become a future pope, to be guide for the Franciscans. The cardinal tried to reason with Francis that a balance had to be struck between his radical vision with its demands and a workable organization that could find a permanent home in the world. The struggle was not new. There is always the conflict between a dreamer's reality and the world's. The new order would have to conform with the whole complex of Christian organizational life of the times. Compromise was inevitable.

The famous Chapter of Mats took place in September of 1221. It was the meeting time of all the members of the order for discussing common concerns. The name came from the rush-fabricated huts quickly set up and for the convening of this general chapter meeting. A revised Rule was read and discussed. Francis held out for his original vision. He shocked his brothers by resigning from the order as leader. They, of course, were distraught and begged him to stay. Francis, however, ended by saying he would be a fool in the world. He began to spend more time in solitude and meditation on the crucified Lord.

If we are willing to hear, Francis challenges us to a painful dimension of prayer. Some of us see clearly the fierce, unfair struggles for power in our secular jobs. If we are able to exert power and find delight in shaping our church, however, we see less clearly the fierce struggles for power in the church. Because we care about the church and have our own special vision and strengths, we can be subtlety caught in power plays with others who also care and have different visions.

Francis demonstrates incredible humility in giving up his power to be head of his order. But his mere presence and faithfulness to his vision continued to be ferment with his order and church. If we dare, we pray for God to help us implement our vision and to acknowledge there are others who may share a different view. We pray for wisdom to discern when we should strongly advance ourselves and our agendas, and when we should allow others the privilege of leadership—when we should be the minority voice.

Lectio Divina

Jesus, knowing that the Father had given all things into his hands, and that he had come from God and was going to God, got up from the table, took off his outer robe, and tied a towel around himself. Then he poured water into a basin and began to wash the disciples' feet, and to wipe them with the towel that was tied around him. (John 13:3-5)

Examen

We all need to express our convictions as members of the church, but we need to ask how we go about exercising power in making our convictions felt. We need to pray for balance: "Lord, give me strength to make my convictions known, and give me courtesy to not impose my will. In fact, grant me the grace to concede to a better argument or way."

Closing Meditation

Those who are set over others should glory only as much in this preferment as they would if they were deputed to the office of washing the feet of the brothers. And if they are more upset when superiority is taken away than they would be at the loss of the office of washing feet, so much the more do they lay up treasures for themselves to the peril of their soul. (Admonitions of St. Francis)[4]

PREPARING FOR A GOOD DEATH

For to me, living is Christ and dying is gain. If I am to live in the flesh, that means fruitful labor for me. . . . My desire is to depart and be with Christ, for that is far better; but to remain in the flesh is more necessary for you. (Phil 1:21-24)

Selah

Francis, ever eager to walk in the steps of Jesus, regarded martyrdom to be a high calling. In his own lifetime, some of his brothers began missionary work abroad and died for their faith. He wished fervently to preach to the Muslims and wage war in his own spiritual way. He would have seen martyrdom to have been a noble end, but this was not to be. He would begin to die after his great vision on Mount Alverna. The process was painful and prolonged. In a way, his prayer to identify with the suffering Lord was answered in full measure.

Murray Bodo, a contemporary Franciscan, understands well the need for spiritual retreat, for "the cave" of Mount Alverna.[5] Identifying with Francis, who died as a middle-aged man at age forty-five, Bodo speaks of people in midlife losing nerve. Dreams of youth seem to have been illusions or incapable of fulfillment.

It is good to burrow deep somewhere, away from the surface definition of reality. The cave is somehow like the soul, a place of dark depths that houses monsters we need to face. We wrestle for the deepest truth, the hardest truth. We wrestle for integrity, keeping faith with the best we have envisioned. Francis had seen his order grow to mammoth size. The Rule was being compromised, and he could no longer shape the group with his intense obedience to his understanding of the gospel.

Two years before his death, Francis made his way again to Mount Alverna. He took a small party of his closest friends. When they reached the top, they built a few huts of tree branches. Something of the life shared there can be understood by looking at the Rule for Hermitages:

> Those who wish to live religiously in hermitages should be three brothers or four at the most. Two of these should be mothers, and they may have two sons or at least one. The two who are mothers should follow the life of Martha, while the two sons should follow the life of Mary and they may have an enclosure in which each one may have his small cell in which he may pray and sleep. And they should always say Compline of the day immediately after sundown, and they should be eager to keep silence, and to say their hours, and to rise for Matins; and let them seek first of all the kingdom of God and his justice.[6]

At first Francis lived and prayed with the brothers. He obviously was the "son" or follower of Mary, and the brothers became his "mothers," performing the work of Martha who made it physically possible for another to have the deepest contemplative experience. Francis was more and more drawn to isolation, to God alone. His brothers respected his distance.

Francis was struggling with the direction of his order. He was praying fervently for the gift of surrender. He could not impose his will on others by force, and the order was in God's hands. He drew closer and closer to the rejected, suffering Jesus. He prayed for a special blessing of identification with his Lord:

> O my Lord Jesus Christ, two graces do I pray thee to grant unto before I die: the first, that while I live I may feel in my body, so far as is possible, that sorrow, sweet Lord, that thou didst suffer in the hour of thy most bitter passion; the second, that I may feel in my heart, so far as may be possible, that exceeding love wherewith, O Son of God, thou was enkindled to endure willingly for us sinners agony so great.[7]

Francis was rewarded with an awesome vision. Christ appeared enfolded by a fiery seraph, and Francis was scarred like Christ with five wounds. Like his Lord of both transfiguration and crucifixion, he had undergone experiences. It was now only a matter of time to return to his heavenly father.

Francis began to take leave of his friends. First he gave a benediction, a farewell blessing, to his beloved brother Leo. The group made its way back to San Damiano where Francis was forced to stop and rest for eight weeks. He was put in simple lodgings outside the monastery. Clare and her sisters were able both to nurse him and to prepare to give him up. He submitted to the will of Brother Elias, now head of his order, to undergo treatment for his ophthalmia. It was a painful and useless operation.

Finally, after a side trip to Siena for another useless medical treatment, Francis and his group went home to the Portiuncula. He said goodbye to his beloved Assisi and wrote his last will and testament. This last will was the clear declaration again that to follow Christ was a radical call to discipleship. He did not approve of the laxity that was coming into his order. He did not approve of those who made free interpretations of clear instructions to live a life of absolute simplicity and obedience to the gospel.

> This is how the Lord gave me, Brother Francis, the grace to begin to do penance; when I was yet in my sins, it seemed to me unbearably bitter to see lepers. And the Lord himself led me among them, and I showed kindness toward them. And as I went away from them, that which had seemed bitter to me was now changed for me into sweetness of mind and body. And then I tarried yet a little while, and left the world.
>
> And the Lord gave me such a faith in the churches, that in a simple way I would thus pray and say: We adore you, O Lord Jesus Christ, and in all your churches which are in the whole world, and we bless you because by your holy cross you have redeemed the world.
>
> And those who came to accept this way of life gave to the poor whatever they might have had. And they were content with one habit, quilted inside and out, with a cord and breeches. And we had no desire for aught else. . . . And we were without learning, and subject to all. And I was wont to work with my hands, and I still wish to do so.
>
> And all my Brothers, both clerics and laics, I firmly charge by obedience not to make any explanation of the Rule or of these words and say: "Thus they are to be understood." Rather, as the Lord has granted me simply and plainly to speak and write the Rule and these words, so simply and without gloss you are to understand them, and carry them out by your holy deeds to the end.[8]

As death came nearer, Francis had one last instruction for his friends. He asked to be stripped naked, laid on mother earth, and left to God. Again we see his desire to strip himself constantly of all pretension and protection, to be surrendered completely to God. He died October 3, 1226. The world grieved, and within two years the Church canonized him as a saint.

I believe we can gain enormous help from Francis in checking our ambition, whether it be within the church or in the world. Of course, we need to have drive and advocate our causes and convictions, but praying within his mode we can be made sensitive to the subtle power drives that can turn a good person into a manipulator or tyrant.

Francis also enables us to prepare for a midlife reckoning. I am now a middle-aged man, a bit older than Francis was when he died. I understand well how the years take a toll on one's energies and beliefs for a better world. Though he could not change the direction of his order or recover the life of his youthful group, Francis did not compromise his vision. He trusted God to work through the corporate wisdom of the church, even when its decisions were painful for him to bear.

While the order would not duplicate his radical vision, the order also would not deny the power of his radical obedience and simplicity that was bringing renewal into a worldly church. No other person could ever replace Francis; everyone within his movement would forever return to his burning commitment, which in turn took them back to the crucified Lord.

Francis finally prepares us for a good death. We of the modern age have many ways to keep from facing death. I sometimes feel unreal in our funeral homes. With soft, sentimental music playing, with painted corpses made to look "natural," with homilies that deny we are truly separated in a vital way from loved ones, we can postpone the moment of truth. Medieval saints prepared for death from the beginning of their vocations. The coming of death was a summons to make this life count.

In the last will and testament of Francis quoted above, we notice his memory of dealing with lepers. It was a part of his conversion, facing the awful truths of life. Something deep within him was freed once he overcame his fear and revulsion. Lepers force us to see that we cannot be guaranteed a life of security and pleasant arrangements. These isolated souls, still human, need to be loved and can be given quality life if not thrown onto the ash heap.

My wife presently is on an AIDS care team that is connected to a ministry of our church. I feel this is a Franciscan application of the gospel. We are connected to isolated souls, human and sensitive, who need to be loved. They are given quality life in what time is left for them by having friends who touch. And perhaps more importantly, we who seem to give the care are freed from some primordial fear and anxiety. We face the coming of death and see it as a summons to make this life count.

Lectio Divina

Just as we have borne the image of the man of dust, we will also bear the image of the man of heaven. What I am saying, brothers and sisters, is this: flesh and blood cannot inherit the kingdom of God, nor does the perishable inherit the imperishable. (1 Cor 15:49-50)

Examen

Many of us avoid thoughts of our own mortality, but we can often sense the presence of a living Lord who is far from dead. Our hope is our connection to this resurrected Lord. We need to connect to people who need comfort as they face dying. It prepares us for death and the next dimension.

Closing Meditation

Praised be my Lord, through our sister Bodily Death, from whom no living person can escape. Woe to those who die in mortal sin! But blessed are those found in your most holy will, for the second death will do them no harm. (The Canticle of Brother Sun)[9]

Notes

[1] *The Little Flowers of St. Francis,* Everyman's Library (New York: Dutton, 1973) 58-59.

[2] *The Writings of St. Francis,* trans. Ignatius Brady (Assisi: Casa Editrice Francescana, C.E.F.A., 1989) 138-40.

[3] Murray Bodo, *Through the Year with Francis of Assisi: Daily Meditations from His Words and Life* (New York: Image Books of Doubleday, 1987) 44.

[4] Brady, 110.

[5] Bodo, 47-50.

[6] "The Rule of the Friars Minor," *Francis and Clare: The Complete Works, The Classics of Western Spirituality* (New York: Paulist, 1982) 147.

[7] John Moorman, *St. Francis of Assisi* (London: SPCK, 1963) 106-107.

[8] *The Writings of St. Francis,* 143-47.

[9] Brady, 20.

❧5❧
PRAYING WITH FRANCIS TODAY

If I speak in the tongues of mortals and of angels, but do not have love, I am a noisy gong or a clanging cymbal. And if I have prophetic powers, and understand all mysteries and all knowledge, and if I have all faith, so as to remove mountains, but have not love, I am nothing. If I give away all my possessions, and if I hand over my body so that I may boast, but do not have love, I gain nothing.

Love is patient; love is kind; love is not envious or boastful or arrogant or rude. It does not insist on its own way; it is not irritable or resentful; it does not rejoice in wrongdoing, but rejoices in the truth. It bears all things, believes all things, hopes all things, endures all things. . . .

Now I know only in part; then I will know fully, even as I have been fully known. And now faith, hope, and love abide, these three; and the greatest of these is love. (1 Cor 13)

Selah

These words of Paul describe well how Francis and Lady Julian understood life in Christ. Though they accepted hard disciplines of piety, they both focused on the grace of God and not on their own merits. They were love mystics who shared a burning devotion to their Lord. He was treasured as their human brother and divine son of God. They help us see how the loving Christ and the New Testament witness are incarnated again and again.

At this point, I would like to share from my personal pilgrimage things I have learned from Francis. During the late 1980s, I became a third order Franciscan with the Anglicans in Hong Kong. The bishop gave permission for a Baptist missionary to be an official part of the group. Our group was extremely small, so fellowship was rich. My spiritual director was an Australian lawyer who had grown up in a strict, Protestant fundamentalist sect. As he moved out of his childhood church into a more inclusive church, he found great inspiration from Francis, liberator of so many of us.

It was an interesting discipline for my Anglican friends with very good incomes to speak of Franciscan simplicity. We tried to go through Francis back to the Christ of the Gospels to find a way to live a holy life in secular, bustling Hong Kong. I learned from Francis to strive for radical simplicity and live within my heritage and faith family.

PRAYING FOR SIMPLICITY AND JOY

The kingdom of heaven is like treasure hidden in a field, which someone found and hid; then in his joy he goes and sells all that he has and buys that field. (Matt 13:44)

Selah

There is nothing wonderful about living in grinding poverty. Poverty dehumanizes rich and poor alike. The poor can feel trapped, worthless, enraged, then deadened. The rich can feel correct, condescending, even chosen and blessed by God. What do we make then of Francis idealizing Lady Poverty? He is speaking of a radical simplicity, of enjoying the basics of life and rejecting a greedy spirit. He was a rich man's son and had a choice.

Out of this radical simplicity came all the virtues of Francis. It characterized his obedience, chastity, and service. He was obedient to Christ as he discovered him in scripture, mother church, and personal experience. He did not appreciate the proud scholars who boasted of their intellectual gifts nor trust them to give proper understanding of Christian life. He read the Scripture rather literally. The Psalms were his own cries of lament and praise. The instructions of Jesus to his disciples were his own marching orders.

I have spent all my life as a theological student and teacher. I have experienced enormous liberation because of the opportunity to do serious study, but I have never forgotten that my living experience with God began in a small church as a child. I lived among farm people with modest educational backgrounds who took scripture very seriously. As a child, I learned to pour over the Bible, and I preached to my father's cornfields. I believe we must learn that delicate balancing act of reading critically and reading reverently. Francis is a constant reminder not to make our faith too complicated or to be paralyzed by analysis.

For Francis, celibacy was the obvious best way to be chaste. He and his brothers needed to be free in a maximum way. They could construct simple rush huts and not worry about adequate protection for families. They could move at any time on preaching tours throughout Europe. Celibacy was a way to achieve a higher level of simplicity. And, of course, it pleased Francis to imitate literally his Lord Jesus, a celibate itinerant evangelist.

Francis had to deal with his own eros, however. He learned an appropriate way to channel his feelings for women. He received from Lady Clare and the sisters at San Damiano enormous affection and support. He was not afraid of being a man with motherly responsibilities. In his Rule he sometimes speaks of the brothers who are to act as mothers. Like many pastors, I have known great enabling through women in the churches who loved me and their church. And I have been made sensitive to the motherly dimension found in all caregivers.

Francis never separated his adoration of God from service to his fellows. His prayers and worship gave him an overwhelming sense of the grandeur of God and his own nothingness without God. He was a beggar who found some food and wanted to share it with other beggars. For him it was inconceivable that the church should be an arena for personal glory. It was not a way to find power, glory, and wealth, all covered over with a veneer of piety. He shook his church with its powerful prelates and worldly priests. He called his church back to gospel simplicity, to the Sermon on the Mount, to the warnings of Jesus against trusting wealth. He identified with the Jesus who gave hope to the marginalized, victimized, the poor.

Many of the churches of North America are large and wealthy. They easily entrench the political values of their privileged members. It is an eternal battle to be an inclusive church, to live with the constant dynamic of receiving someone not of the same background or experience. There is always need of the prophet and poet, someone like Francis, to call us back to ministering to the poor as we remember we all are poor.

I have found encouragement in reading of a Franciscan who works with the churches of South America. Leonardo Buff is a liberation theologian who is committed to building up a church of the poor for the poor. Working within a culture that has been penetrated by Catholic witness for centuries, he has his own particular kind of problems. His church, the Catholic church, became identified with the rich and powerful. Yet that same church produces its own prophets who give hope to the voiceless and poor. A constant stream of martyrs from South America presses the claims of a radical gospel simplicity. All people are beloved children of God and must be given dignity, a chance for a decent life, and a voice.[1]

As a seminary student, I was mesmerized by reading Albert Schweitzer. The conclusion of his famous book, *Quest for the Historical Jesus,* left me for many years with a kind of vague faith. He correctly argued that the modern studies of the life of Jesus were all flawed. We all make Jesus into our own best image. But we can follow him in a mystical kind of way. As we try to serve our fellows, Jesus begins to take shape. This is all true, to a point.

In the past few years I have found that my identification with Franciscan souls has dispelled much of my earlier vagueness. Francis looked at the baby Jesus and rejoiced. He listened to the teacher Jesus and obeyed. He knelt at the cross of Jesus and wept. He did not turn his experience into Platonizing concepts. He simply was in the presence of a friend. If I have learned how to love wife, children, and colleagues without having complete knowledge of my own psyche or theirs, surely I can learn to love the Christ by simply being in his presence.

Lectio Divina

But the Lord answered her, "Martha, Martha, you are worried and distracted by many things; there is need of only one thing. Mary has chosen the better part, which will not be taken away from her." (Luke 10:41-42)

Examen

We can be too impressed with the complexity of life and end up in moral paralysis. Though hard to implement, the gospel has a simple core. We simply love with all our capacity God and our fellows. In the midst of loving identification, we sometimes suffer but always know joy and great hope. Let us pray for simplicity of intention.

Closing Meditation

When the sweetest melody of spirit would flame up in his heart, he would release it by singing in French, and the trickle of divine inspiration which his inner ear had caught would begin to overflow like a minstrel's song. At times, as I have seen with my own eyes, he would pick up a stick from the ground and, holding it on his left arm, would draw across it another stick bent by means of a string, as if he were playing the violin. Then pretending to play, he would sing in French the praises of the Lord. (Celano, Second Life, 127)[2]

PRAYING IN COMMUNITY

Therefore, since we are surrounded by so great a cloud of witnesses, let us lay aside every weight and the sin that clings so closely, and let us run with perseverance the race that is set before us, looking to Jesus the pioneer and perfecter of our faith, who for the sake of the joy that was set before him endured the cross, disregarding its shame, and has taken his seat at the right hand of the throne of God. (Heb 12:1-2)

Selah

Francis was driven by an inner fire, a spirit that longed to come closer and closer to God and his purity. He was consumed by the joy and the summons of God's love. He is good illustration of the saying "To see the face of God is to die." Of course, his high expectations could not endure the institutionalization he had to follow. Later revisions of his simple Rule would relax his stringent requirements. Many persons could not imitate his lifestyle. He could not mold the lives of thousands who filled his three orders before his death.

But Francis did have support systems, and they were magnificent. I mention three: an inner circle of disciples, Lady Clare and her order, and Lady Mary and the hosts of heaven. Francis found great delight in those who first followed him. The little band provided enormous moral support.

The first two to join Francis and embrace simplicity were men of consequence in the world. Bernard Quintavalle was a rich and prominent citizen of Assisi. Peter of Catania was a jurist; some texts called him a cathedral canon. He was a graduate of the university in Bologna, famous for its study of law.

People such as Bernard were devoted to Francis. The story of Bernard testing Francis illustrates the intense and simple prayer life of Francis. He invited Francis to spend the night in his home. After retiring, Bernard pretended to be asleep, though he planned to see what Francis would do. Thinking he was unobserved, Francis slipped out of bed, knelt to pray, and spent the evening repeating a wondrous cry of love, "My God, My God."

Perhaps the brother closest to Francis was Leo. He joined the order in 1210 and was with both Francis and Clare when they died. He became confessor, secretary, and constant companion to Francis in his last years. There are only two extant pieces of writing from Francis, one of which is a note written to Leo. Francis praised his purity of soul and great simplicity. He often comforted Leo when his tender conscience was pricked. The two enabled each other to maintain their high calling.

No treatment of Francis should ignore the place of Clare. When I visited Assisi, I received certain impressions that do not come with mere reading. I not only was overwhelmed by the beauty of the place, but also by two large basilicas in the city. One is dedicated to Francis; one to Clare. At the time I visited the city, the basilica for Clare also housed the large, old Byzantine cross that was Christ's medium for speaking to Francis. Memorabilia from the lives of the two saints are in the basilica. It seems a fitting arrangement since their lives were intertwined in mutual sacrifice.

Clare was from an aristocratic family and destined to be married off to a powerful man to enhance the family fortunes. She was eleven years younger than Francis and was bound to have heard him preach in Assisi. Like many followers, she became drawn to the new life that Francis offered. She defied her parents and ran away to the Portiuncula, seeking refuge from parents and the opportunity to live in evangelical poverty like Francis. She was taken to San Damiano, site of the speaking cross that had moved Francis. This became her home and that of other women who flocked to her as spiritual mother. She remained in this same dwelling for forty-two years, from 1212 (the year of her flight) to 1253 (the year of her death).

Thirteenth-century Italy had no place for female itinerant evangelists. Women who were called like Francis would have had to find a special ministry. Francis was forced to organize a way for Clare and those who followed her to live out their vocation. Clare became the mother superior of an enclosed order dedicated to a life of intercessory prayer. We have surviving letters she wrote to pious noblewomen in Europe, such as the letter to Blessed Agnes of Prague, daughter of the king of Bohemia. Wherever Francis traveled, he knew that he was continuously being held up in prayer by Clare and the ladies of San Damiano.

Besides the prayer support of earthly friends, Francis felt very empowered by the hosts of heaven. God provided comfort not only through earthly friends, but also through protecting angels and saints who lived with God and shared his concerns. Francis had great love for Mary, mother of Jesus and queen of heaven. He shared the medieval notion of Mary gracing the masculine court of God. But Francis also had a healthy regard for the humanity of Mary, just as he did for the humanity of Jesus. If he honored Mary, he did so because she enabled him to love Christ more fully.

PRAYING WITH THE SAINTS

I believe Catholics need to hear the warning note from their Protestant brothers and sisters in regard to Marian devotion, and Protestants need to hear from Catholic friends how Mary can be a means to draw closer to Christ. Below are two examples of how Francis included Mary in his prayer life. She was to be honored for being home to Christ, and we are to be like Mary by being a mothering agent for God's love.

To Mary and All the Holy Virtues

Hail his palace, hail his tabernacle, his house. Hail his vesture, hail his handmaid, his mother. And hail all you holy virtues, who through the grace and illumination of the Holy Spirit are poured into the hearts of believers, so that you might transform unfaithfulness into faithfulness to God.[3]

From Letter to the Faithful

We are mothers of our Lord Jesus Christ when we carry him in our hearts and in our bodies, lovingly, and with a pure and sincere conscience, and give birth to him through the working of his grace in us which should shine forth as an example to others.[4]

Francis learned lessons through hard experience. His experiences can strengthen our lives of prayer and thus our relationships to God and others. We pray to be spared the illusion that wealth is an adequate base for a meaningful life. We pray for patience to allow God to deepen our conversion and reveal a way for us to serve him. We seek support from others who understand and share our journey. Our friends surely include those living here and now and those whose influence lives beyond the grave.

Blessed are the poor in spirit, for theirs is the kingdom of heaven. (Matt 5:3)

Lectio Divina

No one has greater love than this, to lay down one's life for one's friends. You are my friends if you do what I command you. I do

108

not call you servants any longer, because the servant does not know what the master is doing; but I have called you friends, because I have made known to you everything that I have heard from my Father. (John 15:13-15)

Examen

While we need times of solitude and deep personal soul searching, we also need times of connecting with friends. Jesus is our model. He had isolated periods of prayer. He also bonded with friends and found support in their company. He has called us "friend." Meditate on Christ as friend and those who have incarnated him as friends.

Closing Meditation

I had never entertained the slightest thought of living alone. I was made for companions; I was made for community. From the very beginning of my conversion to God, I sensed that there would be many to follow me, since the road I had found was beautiful, and so was the joy that the gospel of Jesus gave me. . . . What sweetness in the thought of my companions in faith! They seemed to be madmen. Whenever we met, we would run through the meadows like little boys, singing, drunk with the gladness of the gospel. We lived like skylarks. Our true prayer was joy. Our true rule was the gospel and the certainty that God was guiding us.[5]

A SUMMONS TO WALK AND PRAY

I enjoin all my brothers, be they clerics or laics, whether they go through the world or reside somewhere, that they have no beast of burden, either with them, or in the keeping of others, or any other way. Nor are they permitted to ride horseback unless they are constrained by infirmity or great necessity. (Franciscan Rule of 1221)[6]

Selah

Perhaps we can change a whole generation and a whole society by beginning with our own discipline of praying and by taking walks. When we take walks, we can really look at what unfolds around us, think on the great mothering love of God that has called us all into being. We look at all levels of God's creation—humankind, our animal "brothers and sisters," and the "brothers and sisters of nature."

Walking took a large part of the time of Francis and his itinerant brothers. In fact, Francis forbade his brothers to ride donkeys unless they were ill. Brother donkey could be asked to bear merchandise in the businesses of men or supplies for his brothers, but walking was best for people. After all, God equipped us with legs to walk and eyes to see a wondrous world unfold that comes particularly alive with walking.

Walking with friends is a particular pleasure. Though all of God's creation has something of God's own life, only men and women have a conscious capability of understanding. Walking with companions is opportunity to double the awareness of how rich God's world really is. Conversations can easily be prayers, though not necessarily couched in liturgical terms. Thoughts can be provoked that can be recovered in later private times of meditation and expression.

We must not take ourselves too seriously. A look at the animal world gave Francis a touch of humor and knowledge. Francis called his body Brother Ass. He asked Brother Ass to forgive him for so burdening it. He likened himself to a lark, called "cowled lark" by common folk. The bird wore the color worn by his brothers. The bird seemed to have a cowl over its head like the brothers. The lark went down the road to see what food could be found. The lark flew freely through the air, rejoicing in the goodness of God's creation. The lark is a humble bird, providing a suitable lesson to all good brothers:

> Thus she offers the religious an example of how not to wear elegant, flashy clothes, but moderately priced things, of the color of earth, the humblest of the elements.[7]

In walking, we can become aware of what is most taken for granted. Francis had a keen awareness of water, stones, wood, and flowers. His mind saturated with scripture and his soul saturated with the love of God drew continuous parallels between natural and spiritual phenomena. When he walked over stones, he spoke with reverence of the one who in scripture is called "The Rock." When he washed his hands in a stream, he remembered the water of holy baptism. When he prepared a fire, he was careful not to destroy a whole tree. When a brother planted a garden, he asked him to leave room for flowers.[8]

Many people have a statue of Francis in their yards or flower gardens, an appropriate way to remember the saint. It is even better to take on the discipline of daily walks to relax the body and mind, to begin to see nature as mother earth and to meditate on the inexhaustible, creating love of God.

Lectio Divina

They heard the sound of the Lord God walking in the garden at the time of the evening breeze, and the man and his wife hid themselves from the presence of the Lord God among the trees of the garden. (Gen 3:8)

Examen

We have a marvelous picture of God in human form in the Garden of Eden. According to this story, God took time out to take walks with Adam and Eve. Imagine in your next walk that God is walking beside you. Share with God the news of the day.

Closing Meditation

Often, without moving his lips, St. Francis would meditate for a long time, and concentrating, centering his external powers, he would rise in spirit to heaven. Thus, he directed his whole mind and affections to the one thing he was asking of God. He was not then so much a man who prayed, as a man who had become a living prayer. (Celano, Second Life, 95)[9]

Notes

[1]Leonardo Buff, *St. Francis: A Model for Human Liberation* (London: SCM, 1986). I call attention particularly to Chapter 2, "Preferential Option for the Poor," 48-80.

[2]Murray Bodo, *Through the Year with Francis of Assisi: Daily Meditations from His Words and Life* (New York: Image Books of Doubleday, 1987) 160-61.

[3]Ibid., 94.

[4]Ibid., 95.

[5]Carlo Carretto, *I, Francis* (London: William Collins, 1982) 48.

[6]Bodo, 83.

[7]Ibid., 174.

[8]*The Little Flowers of St. Francis*, Everyman's Library (New York: Dutton, 1973) 293.

[9]Bodo, 139.